Never Mind the Sizzle...
Where's the Sausage?

By the same author

The Brand Gym: A practical workout for boosting brand and business
Brand Stretch: Why 1 in 2 extensions fail and how to beat the odds
Brand Vision: How to energize your team to drive business growth

A Brand Gym book, by David Nichols

Return on Ideas: A practical guide to making innovation pay

Never Mind the Sizzle... Where's the Sausage?

Branding based on substance not spin

David J. Taylor

John Wiley & Sons, Ltd

Other Wiley Editorial Offices

John Wiley & Sons Inc., 111 River Street, Hoboken, NJ 07030, USA

Jossey-Bass, 989 Market Street, San Francisco, CA 94103-1741, USA

Wiley-VCH Verlag GmbH, Boschstr. 12, D-69469 Weinheim, Germany

John Wiley & Sons Australia Ltd, 42 McDougall Street, Milton, Queensland 4064,
Australia

John Wiley & Sons (Asia) Pte Ltd, 2 Clementi Loop #02-01, Jin Xing Distripark,
Singapore 129809

John Wiley & Sons Canada Ltd, 6045 Freemont Blvd, Mississauga, ONT, L5R 4J3,
Canada

Wiley also publishes its books in a variety of electronic formats. Some content that
appears in print may not be available in electronic books.

Anniversary Logo Design: Richard J. Pacifico

A catalogue record for this book is available from the British Library and the Library
of Congress.

ISBN 13: 978-1-84112-769-9

Typeset in 11/16 pt Swiss 721 by Thomson Digital
Printed and bound in Great Britain by TJ International Ltd, Padstow, Cornwall

This book is printed on acid-free paper responsibly manufactured from sustainable
forestry in which at least two trees are planted for each one used for paper production.

Substantial discounts on bulk quantities of Capstone Books are available to
corporations, professional associations and other organizations. For details
telephone John Wiley & Sons on (+44) 1243-770441, fax (+44) 1243 770571 or
email corporatedevelopment@ wiley.co.uk

A Jessica,
Tu seras toujours ma princesse

Contents

Thank you…

The idea for writing a story that smuggles in branding tips and tricks has been banging around in my head ever since I worked as a Brand Manager at P&G, and that's longer ago than I'm prepared to admit. Back then, I found that telling stories was one of the best ways of training new brand managers. This was because brand success, or failure, was down to *how* people did stuff as much as *what* they did. So, the first hearty thank you is to John Moseley at Capstone for backing my belief that there was a market for an entertaining, accessible book on branding. He has hedged his bets by saying that WTS? will either be a huge hit, or a total flop. Let's hope for both our sakes that the first of these is right.

Second, thanks to all the readers of wheresthesausage.com who have helped make this one of the first books to be 'co-created' via a blog (very 'Web 2.0' eh?). Over 100 people voted on the best cover, and the winner has taken its rightful place on the book in your hands. But special thanks go to those who spent time reading the first draft and giving feedback. Bob Hogg did the Simpton's organization chart. Rebecca, you should find a clearer explanation for Hugo's brand ego-tripping. Rob, hopefully

I've fixed the mistakes your eagle eyes picked up. Simon, I tightened up the first three chapters, cutting out 10–15% of the content to speed things up (for a writer, this is like chopping off one of your own arms!). Nick, I used your feedback to write an Introduction that made it clear who the book was for. Alan, thanks for loving it and calling it a 'masterpiece', providing a welcome pick-me-up on a day I was bogged down.

Finally, thanks to my brilliant business partner David Nichols. One of his many talents is writing musicals, and he used these skills in helping craft the story. WTS? was always meant to be a business book first, and a story second, but I did want it to be an entertaining read. He helped keep the tension going in the second half of the book, and this will hopefully keep you reading right to the end. Oh, and if you like or loathe the bit of love interest, that was Anne-Marie's idea, not mine.

Introduction – let me tell you a story...

Where's the Sausage? (WTS?) is for people looking for practical, action-oriented ideas about brand building in an accessible, entertaining format. It's written to be read in a couple of hours, ideal for your next short-haul flight or train trip. In contrast to most other books on branding, WTS? is written not as a classic textbook, but in the form of a (hopefully) fun and involving story. There are bags of bite-sized insights, tips and tricks, but these are 'smuggled' into the story. You will follow a year in the life of our hero, Bob Jones, as he tries to get to grips with brand management at Simpton's Sausages. Bob and the other characters are explained in the organisation chart opposite. He stumbles over loads of brand examples, both good and bad, and scribbles down little tools and checklists that you can apply to your own brand.

Chances are you will either love or hate the whole story thing, based on the feedback from guinea pig readers recruited via the wheresthesausage.com blog. Most found it easy to read and fun; but others didn't get into it, and said they would prefer a straightforward textbook. If you're in the latter camp, you may want to put this book back on the shelf, or click back online, and consider one of the four more serious brandgym books that cover brand vision, stretch and innovation. But if you're up for a business story that takes a light-hearted look at brand management, then please read on. The characters and situations might be exaggerated to make them more interesting... but if you're honest, are they that far from the truth?!

The book is ideal for branding 'virgins', including those sceptics put off up to now by too much jargon and too many buzzwords. It is also for more experienced people, who want a refresher on the principles of building brands on substance, not spin.

There are 18 brand stories in the book, and where you see **part of the text underlined** you can get more details by

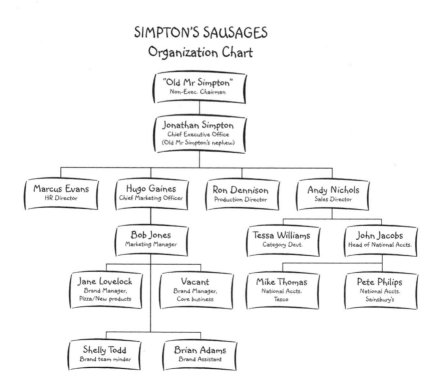

SIMPTON'S SAUSAGES
Organization Chart

"Old Mr Simpton"
Non-Exec. Chairman

Jonathan Simpton
Chief Executive Office
(Old Mr Simpton's nephew)

Marcus Evans
HR Director

Hugo Gaines
Chief Marketing Officer

Ron Dennison
Production Director

Andy Nichols
Sales Director

Bob Jones
Marketing Manager

Tessa Williams
Category Devt.

John Jacobs
Head of National Accts.

Jane Lovelock
Brand Manager,
Pizza/New products

Vacant
Brand Manager,
Core business

Mike Thomas
National Accts.
Tesco

Pete Philips
National Accts.
Sainsbury's

Shelly Todd
Brand team minder

Brian Adams
Brand Assistant

visiting the blog at wheresthesausage.com. Here you will find TV adverts, packaging, market data and much more. Please do add a comment or two at the end of the posts you visit. This linkage between a business book and a blog is the first of its kind as far as I know.

Quarter One

BRANDING FOR BUSINESS

1.

January – The buzzword battle begins (don't be blinded by the jargon)

WHAT HAVE I DONE TO DESERVE THIS? (MONDAY, JANUARY 1, 2007)

It's official: I'm stuffed. As stuffed as the gigantic Christmas turkey we finally finished at lunch. Tomorrow I start the first day of my one-year assignment as a Brand Director at Simpton's Sausages. But how can I direct a brand when I don't even understand what one is in the first place? The heavy tome that was supposed to save me has turned out to only darken my depression. My good wife Claire's heart was in the right place when she offered me *Strategic Branding* as a Christmas present, but it might as well be written in the native language of the French author. 450 pages of jargon-heavy gobbledygook, full of complicated, impenetrable diagrams and models. I gave up after page 10 and polished off the latest John Grisham bestseller instead.

And so here I am, making the first entry in my brand new blog, as the digital clock on my PC glows its way inexorably towards midnight. The blogging software was another yuletide gift, this time from my nephew Techno Tim. On one of his rare visits out of his bedroom he drawled that I was, like, totally Victorian to be still writing a diary, as he simultaneously sent a text message from his phone, watched MTV and listened to his iPod.

Well, the big fat branding book will come in handy for one thing: smashing over the head of Marcus Evans from Human Resources. He was the one who gate-crashed my end-of-year performance review to announce that I was to become a 'CROFTer': a cross-functional transferee. In today's complex business world, it was no longer enough for me to excel in my specialist 'silo'. I had to storm the organizational barricades and familiarize myself with another functional area. So, my 14 years of slog spent as a sales rep and then battling with the buyers from Tesco were not going to pay off with me being crowned as Sales Director.

Instead, Marcus primly pronounced – like a vicar reading the Sunday sermon – that I would be spending a year in marketing, or rather 'brand management' as it is now called. When I said there was no way I was spending a year with that bunch of Oxbridge educated, over-intellectual time-wasters, Marcus' shaven head bobbed up and down inside his black polo neck jumper. Unfortunately, my boss Andy Nichols failed to back me up as expected. Seems his wife wanted a tennis court to add to the swimming pool at their villa on the Algarve, and he needed another good year at Simpton's before he could take retirement. I swear he was swallowing back a chortle as he told me that I would be in charge of launching the sausage pizza, the laughing stock of the whole sales department. But he did assure me that the Sales Director's job was mine in a year's time, as long as I didn't screw up as a CROFTer. As I drove home the immortal words of the Pet Shop Boys rang in my ears, as they continue to do now: 'What have I, what have I, what have I done to deserve this?'

NEW KID ON THE BLOCK (TUESDAY, JANUARY 2)

Got to the office at 7.30am to show how keen I was to start CROFTing, but found the marketing area as deserted as the Marie Celeste. Whilst I waited for my new team-mates to arrive, I read the 'Superbrands' supplement from last weekend's *Sunday Times*. It seems that everyone and everything wants to be a brand these days, from pet food to political parties. However, there was no place for Simpton's Sausages in the list of top 100 brands, as voted for by the British public. With £100 million of sales we're bigger than many of the brands who did make it, but it seems we're less loved than McDonald's, KFC and Imodium.

The Simpton's brand management team started to arrive at 9am, with punctuality seemingly inversely proportional to level of seniority. First in was Shelly, the brand 'minder', who was carrying a well-thumbed copy of *Hello!* in one hand and a Starbucks caramel frappuccino in the other. Next in was the brand assistant, Brian Adams, who bore no resemblance whatsoever to the singer. He was tall and gangly like a basketball player and sported black-rimmed glasses. He shyly said hello before sitting down in front of the biggest computer screen I'd ever seen. My brand manager, Jane Lovelock, came rushing in at 9.30am, sucking up files, papers and pizza boxes from her desk like a tornado, a Mont Blanc pen gripped tightly between her teeth. She violently nodded her welcome before rushing off again. And then, on the stroke of 10am, entered my new boss, Hugo Gaines. He sported the same shaven head and black polo neck as Marcus, and looked like he would be more at home in a trendy advertising agency than a sausage company. Seems he and Marcus have known each other since studying together at Oxford. Absolutely flipping fabulous. With a furrowed brow, and not even the slightest hint of irony, Hugo welcomed me onto the 'white-knuckle ride that was the transformation of Simpton's into a truly iconic brand of the 21st century'. I thought about mentioning the fact that we were lagging behind Micky D's, KFC and Imodium in the Superbrand table, but bit my tongue. Hugo announced in his plummy voice that the key task for the day was an in-depth brand briefing lunch up in London at his club, Soho House.

I was surprised to see that Hugo signed in at Soho House as Creative Director of the Hugbrands agency. Seems you can't become a member if you're in charge of marketing sausages. Lunch only served to darken my already gloomy mood, and when the waiter came to take my order I felt like asking for a translator. Hugo had obviously digested all of *Strategic Branding* and many other management books, as he spewed out sentence after sentence of unintelligible brand-speak.

In a nutshell, I think Hugo's strategy boils down to two things, or 'strategic thrusts' as he called them. First, we're going to 'leverage and stretch the brand' by launching a range of new sausage pizzas. The pizzas will use Italian sausages such as salami and chorizo, rather than traditional British ones. Second, we're going to 're-brand' Simpton's with a new 'identity' developed by one of London's trendiest design agencies, which I think means a new logo. This would be announced with a fanfare by a mould-breaking new advertising campaign being created by one of London's trendiest communication agencies. When I asked if this wasn't a bit radical for a brand built on being the best British banger, Hugo almost choked on his third glass of Chilean Chardonnay. He explained that we had to 'jettison this brand baggage so we could take the brand into the 21st century'.

After lunch Hugo left for an important meeting at the agency, so I took the train back to the office by myself and thought about Hugo's strategy. I found it strange that it made no mention at all of the basic product itself. Indeed, the post of Brand Director on the core sausage business was vacant. The other thing missing from my briefing was any mention of the business itself. I knew from my work in sales that the brand was on the rocks, but had expected an in-depth analysis of where the problem areas were. Made a mental note to email Brian for some data on sales and profitability.

DROWNING IN MY BRAND IMMERSION (FRIDAY, JANUARY 5)

Just back from two gruelling days spent in a brand immersion workshop at Babbington House, the country outpost of Hugo's club. There were all five of us from marketing there, although Shelly seemed to spend all her time in the Cowshed Spa. There were also four people from ETC, the communication agency, and another four from INK, the brand identity shop. The workshop was pure hell, with the only good news being that it's the last one I am likely to attend, after the career-limiting comments I made. My behaviour reminded me of my uncle Geoff, who would always embarrass himself by getting completely drunk at family get-togethers and then alternate between cracking rude jokes and noisily breaking wind.

My gaffe came on the first morning, during the scaling of the 'brand pyramid' that was led by Kitty Johansen, the strategic planner from ETC. She was a pencil-thin New Yorker dressed in black from head to toe. Her presentation confirmed my worst fears about branding being one big competition to create the most complicated jargon-heavy diagram possible (Figure 1.1). Kitty started by warning us in hushed tones about how everything was getting faster, smaller and more personal

Figure 1.1: Scaling the brand pyramid

(everything apart from her presentation, that is). She then went on to help us climb up each of the ten levels of branding. She was clearly very proud of the pyramid, giving the impression that ETC had toiled over it for as long as Tutankhamen's team did over his.

I squinted at the pyramid as she talked, trying my best to understand it. Our target consumer would be young, upmarket, urban and active people. This seemed strange, given that our current users were mainly families. Moving up, our products would use top quality ingredients to deliver great taste, which sounded vague. There were a lot more words in the next four

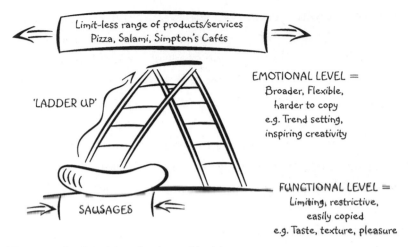

Limit-less range of products/services
Pizza, Salami, Simpton's Cafés

'LADDER UP'

EMOTIONAL LEVEL =
Broader, Flexible,
harder to copy
e.g. Trend setting,
inspiring creativity

SAUSAGES

FUNCTIONAL LEVEL =
Limiting, restrictive,
easily copied
e.g. Taste, texture, pleasure

Figure 1.2: Climbing the brand ladder

layers, which captured the emotional side of the brand. The idea was to forget the boring product bit at the bottom of the pyramid, and 'climb a ladder' up to this emotional level (Figure 1.2), selling a lifestyle, not sausages. We would champion breaking the mould and embracing change, and our 'personality' would be an intoxicating potion of modernity, innovativeness and cosmopolitan flair. According to Kitty, the great thing about working up in this rarefied emotional atmosphere was that we were no longer trapped in sausage-land; we were free to come up with all sorts of sexy new products. Young urbanites would be seduced by our salami pizzas, and then come back to buy stand-alone Simpton's salami. In the future we could open a chain of Simpton's Cafés and sell culinary vacations to Tuscany.

As the presentation reached its climax I became convinced I was on some sort of prankster TV show, with an ex-Big Brother contestant turned presenter about to jump out from behind a potted plant and shout 'You've been had!', ending my misery. Unfortunately, no such respite was at hand, and I watched as Kitty reached brand nirvana right at the top of the pyramid with the 'brand essence'. These two words were supposed to be the distillation of what we wanted the brand to stand for. In hushed tones she announced that our two words were... 'Accessible aspiration!' With a flourish she revealed a huge poster of Kate Moss taking a big bite out of a Simpton's pizza, with what looked like a crowd of scantily clad male strippers from Chippendales hanging at her ankles, begging for a slice. Along the bottom was our new slogan: 'Be Simpsational!'

The end of Kitty's presentation was greeted with rapturous applause, and I did my best to join in. However, a voice inside me kept repeating a phrase over and over again, bursting to explode. Eventually I could hold it in no longer and blurted out: 'Where's the sausage?!' Two by two, twelve admonishing pairs of eyes turned to bore into me. Hugo coughed to clear his throat, and then asked me to explain myself. Rather than shutting up and escaping with only minor injuries, I carried on and asked whether we weren't forgetting the product. Hugo then aimed right below the belt by asking me what sort of branding model I had been taught during *my* MBA, knowing full well I hadn't done one. I mumbled as much, and he suggested that given my lack of experience I had better leave the branding to the experts. I decided to keep my mouth shut for the rest of the day.

The second day saw INK share their latest thinking on the re-branding project, led by their dreadlock-haired hippie-ish creative director, Dave. Rather than simply come up with a new logo, Dave wanted to push the 'creative envelope to breaking point and beyond' by inviting budding young designers to create proposals for the new logo and pizza packaging. The ten best designs would be featured in an exhibition at Tate

Modern and be judged by a panel of leading lights from the music, cinema and art worlds. The ultimate winner would be the future design of Simpton's, appearing on the pizza boxes but also on all other visual materials, such as the sides of lorries and on our website. The team had slaved over a name for the competition and after many hours of deliberation, they thought they had cracked it. With a flourish, the final board was revealed with the title: 'Pizzart'.

Well, if the reaction to Kitty's presentation was rapturous, the response to this one was absolutely orgasmic. Everyone was on their feet giving a standing ovation. When the noise had finally died down Hugo placed the palms of his hands together, his elbows on the table, and rested his fingers on his lips. He rocked gently back and forwards a few times for dramatic effect before telling Dave in hushed tones that his creative proposal was absolutely, totally Simpsational.

The phrase 'Thank God it's Friday' has taken on a whole new meaning for me.

GETTING TO THE BOTTOM LINE (TUESDAY, JANUARY 9)

Today I got an email from Brian with the sales figures I'd asked for. It took him some time to come up with the data as no-one on the brand team had been very interested in detailed financials before. I suppose poring over Excel spreadsheets is not a very Simpsational thing to do.

The numbers made for sorry reading. The profitability of the core sausage business had been in decline for five years, with the brand trapped in a vicious downward cycle of increasing price promotion, leading to less funds for marketing and innovation, leading to less differentiation, more price promotion, and so on. In a way I felt partly responsible for the nightmare we were in, having been part of the sales department's push for more promotional support to protect listings with the key super-market chains such as Tesco, Sainsbury's and Asda-Walmart. At the same time, the supermarkets had been busy developing their 'own label' sausage ranges, such as Tesco Finest and Sainsbury's Taste the Difference.

Simpton's market share had fallen off a cliff, dropping from 35% in 1999 to 19% in 2006. We had been squashed between the competitively priced supermarket brands at one end, and premium gourmet products at the other, from brands like Duchy's Originals and Porkinsons.

Hugo had been brought in a couple of years ago to stop the rot. He sold the company on effectively giving up the core sausage business and seeking salvation in stretching into new areas, starting with the pizza project. His story was that the sausage business was now all about price, so we needed to 'milk' this bit of the business for profit and bet all our market-ing money on the brand extensions. But if premium proposi-tions such as Duchy's had been taking share at the top of the market, was it really all about price I wondered? And when I stopped at Tesco on the way home, I found that their Finest sausages were actually *more* expensive than ours! Weren't we giving up a bit too easily? Against my better judgement I sent an email to Hugo to 'bounce my ideas' off him.

BATTERED, BRUISED BUT STILL ALIVE (MONDAY, JANUARY 22)

Back from a week on a course called 'Courage to change', which involved lots of adventurous outward-bound activities. Several of the attendees ended up in tears, though we were as-sured this was all part of the change-embracing process. How forcing the Finance Director with a fear of heights to jump out of a plane with a parachute on her back will help her implement a computer-based accounting system I really don't know. But then not really knowing what is going on is becoming a recurring theme this year.

Got a predictably terse reply from Hugo to my email on the brand P&L. He said my left-brain focused approach to branding was 'not fully consistent with a holistic, visionary brand transformation process'.

JANUARY'S SUMMARY

1. My worst fears about branding being full of bull and buzzwords have been confirmed.
2. It feels to me like we're neglecting our sausage business with the plans to extend into things like pizza.
3. Will changing the logo on our wrapper really make much difference when the sausages inside stay the same?
4. Everyone seems obsessed with making Simpton's a lifestyle brand. I seem alone in asking 'where's the sausage?'

2.

February – Brand-led business (branding is much more than just a fancy logo)

BRAND IMAGE WRAPPERS (MONDAY, FEBRUARY 5)

It seems that Simpton's are not alone in hoping that a change in design will be enough to save an underperforming business. Take my bank, the Abbey, for example. On Saturday I noticed that the sign outside my local branch had changed. I remembered it being a brightly coloured logo written in lowercase letters; all very nice and warm and friendly. Now it was much more serious and bank-like, with a little red flame.

The funny thing was that once inside nothing much seemed to have changed, apart from the logos on the posters. Same old carpet. Same cheap furniture. And the same bored-looking people behind the counter. I asked the lady serving me about the new 'identity' and what she thought of it. This seemed to make her day, and she laughed her head off. She called it the 'annual makeover', as it was the third change in about as many years. This one was prompted by Abbey being taken over by some big Spanish bank called Salamander. Apparently everyone had been invited to some big fancy show up in town, where the 'nice, helpful people from head office' (not exactly the words she used herself) told them about the latest re-looking. It was all very impressive, like any West End show. However, it was light on any improvements to the branches themselves, or anything for the staff. Exactly the opposite was the case, with 3000 redundancies announced.

It turns out that the Spanish bank is in fact called Santander, who have the funny little red flame as their corporate logo. They had indeed planned to cut 3000 jobs, and to make things worse had later announced that the number would be even higher, at 4000. I also found **the history of the Abbey brand, which had indeed been through many re-designs** (wheresthesausage. com). Each one had been accompanied by bold claims, such as 'Turning banking on its head', but then didn't really seem to deliver much to back these claims up, apart from yet another new logo.

IMPERFECT PIZZA (WEDNESDAY, FEBRUARY 7)

Went on my very first international business trip today, which was all jolly exciting. Hugo, Jane and I jetted off to Milan to visit the supplier of our new sausage pizza. Strangely enough, one of the biggest lessons I learnt was on the journey.

Hugo had booked his car into a valet parking service with British Airways at Heathrow, to avoid the scrum for the short-term car park. As we went to drop the keys off, the guy at the desk greeted Hugo by name before he could even say hello. To check in, we went to a separate 'premium check-in' area, reserved for people flying business and first class, away from the crowds of dawdling pensioners, rowdy teenagers and screaming babies.

And then at the business class lounge, they upgraded Hugo and said we could use the first class lounge as he had a BA Gold Card. Well, when I say we, I mean Hugo and Jane, as he was only allowed one guest. I went to Starbucks, and as I sipped my latte, I scribbled on a napkin the BA approach, and contrasted it with what I'd seen in the Abbey bank. Abbey had re-designed the *outside* of the brand, with a new logo and communication, but the product inside seemed to stay the same. A sort of 'image wrapper' was being used to cover up the product shortcomings. In contrast, **BA had invested in the whole customer experience** (wheresthesausage.com) to have: (i) the valet parking with staff trained up to meet and greet the customer, (ii) a whole separate check-in area for business class customers, (iii) a fantastic business class lounge (at least I assume it was fantastic). My actual experience of BA service was 10 or 20 times more effective than any amount of advertising in making me want to fly with them again, and much harder to copy. The brand was leading the whole business, not just the image wrapper (Figure 2.1).

The business meeting itself was unfortunately more Abbey than BA. The pizza people were all very nice and welcoming, with the big-bellied, bald-headed owner insisting we start by having lunch in the local trattoria. After all, it was almost midday, and Jane did want to oil the rusty Italian she hadn't used since studying it at university. Hugo and Jane enthusiastically took up his offer of trying all three versions of the local wine.

We finally got to the factory at 4pm, which left us exactly half an hour of product sampling before our taxi picked us up for the flight home. I was disappointed not to see a bunch of old ladies hand rolling the pizza base, and putting on fresh tomatoes and a sprinkle of basil. It was a completely industrialized process, capable of producing thousands of pizzas a day.

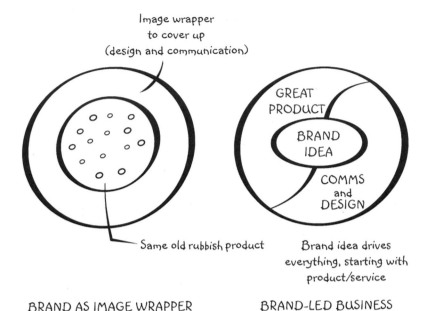

Figure 2.1: Brands built on substance, or spin

Hugo and Jane said they were too full to taste any pizza, but said they looked very nice indeed. I had saved some space, and did some sampling. The pizza was absolutely fine, but confirmed my fears that it was no better than the ones sold by Sainsbury's or Tesco, never mind Pizza Express. With his tongue loosened by the wine, the owner told me that they made product for all the big UK supermarkets, so we'd be amongst good company. So, same factory, same pizza. Just a different wrapper.

OUR VERY OWN IMAGE WRAPPER (FRIDAY, FEBRUARY 9)

Had a meeting with Jane to review some examples of 'mocked up' packaging for the pizzas. There was a whole pile of boxes, each with a different design, but all having in common a loud, garish style and a minute Simpton's logo hidden in the bottom

right corner. She had taken INK's student designer competition idea to a whole new level. Rather than just producing the
winning design, we would market all ten of them as limited edi-
tions, so people could collect the full set. Now, I know from
experience that this works with breakfast cereals offering free
toys for kids, as the cupboard full of uneaten packets shows.
But would this really work with pizza?

I picked up a box for a closer look and asked if there
was anything new about the packaging itself, beyond the
graphic design. Was it easier to open? Did it keep the pizza
fresher for longer? These were clearly questions that had
never crossed Jane's mind. She said that making the pack
better sounded very complicated and would involve working
with the factory, and she hadn't joined brand management
to do that.

I enquired about the price. We would have to sell the pizzas
at £5.50 to make any money, and even then the profit margin
was less than we made on our sausages. We had to pay for
importing the product and then give the supermarkets a hefty
sum to stock the product. They were quite happy selling their
own chilled pizzas, and would only entertain the idea of putting
our new ones on the shelf if they made a very tidy sum from
it. I asked how much Sainsbury's charged for their pizza, and
Jane said she would try and find out. I was sure it was closer
to £3.99.

I summarized where we were. Not only did we have the
same product, from the same factory as the own label pizzas.
We also had the same box. And we were going to be, say,
40% more expensive. But we'd have a nice set of limited edition
designs. And of course, a Simpsational TV advert. For the first
time Jane looked pleased, nodding her head and saying I was
finally getting the hang of brand management.

AT LAST, SIZZLE AND SAUSAGE (WEDNESDAY, FEBRUARY 14)

I fear I am becoming a brandaholic. And to make things worse, my kids are copying me. At breakfast today I started to read the carton of innocent smoothie on the table and found myself laughing out loud. Claire looked up from her muesli and asked me what was so funny, and I explained it was the writing on the pack. The packaging was full of facts but told in a funny, quirky style such as 'We promise that we'll never use any weird stuff in our drinks. And if we do you can tell our Mums'. Even the most banal of instructions were written with a wink of the eye, such as 'Shake before opening, not after'. I could tell from her furrowed brow that she was also starting to fear for the effect that being in marketing was having on my sanity. The kids, however, were interested, and joined me in my pack inspection. Their favourite was the little sentence hidden up in the folds at the top of the carton that read 'email us at iamnosey@innocent. co.uk'. Unfortunately, Amy insisted on taking the pack to show her school friends, which meant her Mum had to pour half the contents down the drain.

The great thing about the innocent smoothie was the way **the stuff on the pack that made me laugh was being used to sell a strong product message** (wheresthesausage.com). I ripped a page out of Amy's reading record notebook and scribbled down an idea. The sizzle was not an add-on, it was being used to promote their sausage (Figure 2.2). The almost child-like innocence of the design and the writing helped get across the idea that the product itself was innocent, by being 100% natural and containing no nasties. This felt better than the 'laddering' I'd learnt about on my fateful trip to Babbington House with the risk of losing touch with the ground, and the product you're selling.

Learnt several interesting things about the innocent brand on Wikipedia, the amazing online encyclopaedia Brian had

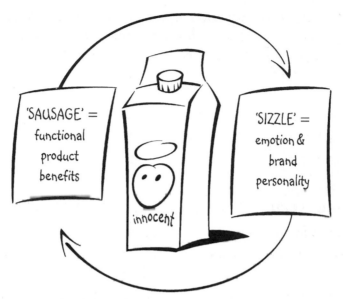

Figure 2.2: Sausage and Sizzle

introduced me to (he's shy, but boy does he know his stuff when it comes to the internet):

- They built a £100 million business, and leading 60% share of the market, *without any advertising!* The business was built on the strength of the product and packaging.
- There's lots of sizzle, but it works with the product story, not separately from it.
- The great product has helped support a price premium versus the supermarkets' copy-cat versions.
- Their brand promise is simple and rooted in the product: 'To make drinks that taste good and do you good without concentrates, preservatives, stabilisers, or any weird stuff'.
- And on their Frequently Asked Questions area, a response to the inquiry I know Amy is about to utter: How are babies made?

When Mummy and Daddy have special hugs, Mummy sometimes whis-
pers a magic word to Daddy. When Daddy hears the magic word, he feels
very happy and in a few seconds they will have ordered a baby, a bit like
shopping on the internet.

Which reminds me. There won't be any 'special hugs' or 'magic words' for me tonight if I don't go out and buy some flowers for Valentine's day.

PUSHING SMOOTHIE UPHILL (MONDAY, FEBRUARY 19)

Armed with my innocent smoothie pack that I stole out of Amy's bedroom whilst she was sleeping, I booked a meeting with Hugo and Jane to share my new-found insights about product-led branding. I suggested we have the meeting at the factory with the product development team to see what innocent-like ideas we could come up with for our sausages. Unfortunately, this was like trying to push a smoothie uphill. I got the distinct impression that Hugo had never been to our sausage factory and had no intention of going there in the near future. Much better to have the product made by a third-party supplier and focus instead on the more important branding stuff like advertising and design.

After the meeting had finished, Jane took me to one side to share a few home truths with me. It seems like the only way you get ahead in marketing is by launching new products such as our pizza project. This allows you to use all the important tools in the branding toolbox (or toys in the toybox), especially advertising and design. But best of all was 'pipeline filling': the product you shipped to the supermarkets at the start of a launch to fill up the shelves. This was a one-off gift from the branding gods; afterwards the only sales made were to replenish packs that were sold each week. And in the case of most new products, this didn't add up to much. Indeed, Jane told me that on average less than 1 in 2 such new launches survived their first year. I suggested that this encouraged you to launch a new product, sell all the initial volume to boost sales figures, bask in the glory for a while and then bugger off. Jane nodded sheepishly.

FIRST TO THE FACTORY (MONDAY, FEBRUARY 26)

Battled my way up the motorway to go and visit our factory just outside Manchester, while Hugo and Jane spent the day at Tate Modern to discuss the brand's design exhibition. I was glad I made the trip; getting an explanation for some of the problems on the brand, and having a chance meeting that might just prove very important indeed.

When I arrived, there was a line-up of six people all waiting to greet me. It seems I was the first person from marketing to come and visit for as long as any of them could remember, so it was a bit of an event. Leading the welcoming committee was Ron Dennison, a gaunt bloke of about 50, whose slicked back hair suggested he was one of Brylcream's last customers. He'd been in charge of product development for 10 years. And for the 15 years before that he had been in production management, working his way up through the ranks. So he had a wealth of experience about the business that I was keen to tap into. His tale was a sorry one, which helped explain the downward sales spiral we were in.

Up until five years ago, Ron's team worked on new recipes and quality improvements; there was a real sense of pride in the product. However, everything changed in 2003 with the retirement of 'Old Mr Simpton', the great, great grandson of Thomas Simpton, who founded the company in 1826. Having no children of his own, Old Mr Simpton reluctantly handed over the reins to his nephew, Jonathan Simpton, who had worked in the City after university, in mergers and acquisitions. He seemed set on pumping up the profits of the company prior to selling it off to private equity investors. It turns out that he was also responsible for hiring Hugo as Marketing Director, after meeting him when doing his MBA at London Business School.

Ron's team were told to stop working on projects to make the products better, and focus instead on cutting costs. By making only small cuts, but lots of them, Jonathan and Hugo thought they could squeeze a lot more profit out of the business. Reluctantly Ron did as he was told, compromising on the quality of the raw materials, adding more filler and less meat, and using artificial preservatives to lengthen the 'shelf-life' of the sausages. However, even if each change was not dramatic, the cumulative effect was; the sausages were now much worse than before. I asked Ron if he could make up some sausages to the pre-Hugo recipe so I could taste the difference for myself.

We went for lunch in the canteen, which was actually very nice. A bit spartan, yes, and no trendy furniture like in London. And they could have done with a few plants and pictures to brighten it up. But I liked the friendly banter of the factory workers, who had obviously known each other for years. I wondered what they would do if Jonathan Simpton achieved his goal of selling the business to a buyer whose first act would probably be to sack most of them in the search for 'cost synergies'.

Ron had to rush off to sort out some problem with one of the production lines, leaving me alone with my musings, when my chance meeting happened. An old chap in a scruffy suit and a white beard asked if he could sit next to me, which was surprising as most of the tables in the canteen were by now free. He asked what my first impressions of the factory were. Thinking he was perhaps someone from the accounts department, or one of Ron's team, I pulled no punches in telling him about my concerns regarding the cuts in product quality and the extension into pizzas. The man nodded sagely as I spoke, seemingly in agreement with my diatribe. He leaned back on his chair and stroked his beard. I enquired about which bit of the company he worked in, to which he replied with a smile and a twinkle in the eye, 'Oh, most of it'. When he saw the confused look on my face he explained that he was Old Mr Simpton. I started to apologize for my comments, feeling that I had just dug another few spades of earth out of the ever-deepening grave of my brand management career. However, he interrupted me to say he agreed wholeheartedly with what I had said, and just wished that his buffoon of a nephew had one tenth of the common sense that I did. He excused himself politely, as he had to prepare for the board meeting that he still ran as non-executive chairman. Seems he has lunch in the factory canteen most days of the week, and hoped to perhaps see me again.

FEBRUARY'S SUMMARY

1. The brand should drive the whole business, not just the image wrapper of communication and brand identity.
2. A new logo can't cover up the shortcomings of a poor product.
3. Emotional sizzle should work *with* the sausage of product benefits to reinforce them, not separately from them.
4. Cut the quality of the product and consumers will catch you out in the end.

3.

March – Elastic brands (stretch your brand too far and it snaps)

HUGO'S BALLS (TUESDAY, MARCH 6)

There were two big things that had been bugging me since my Babbington House briefing from hell. The first was the reliance on advertising spin to build the brand, and I feel like I'm getting to the bottom of that. The other concern is entering the pizza market when our core sausage business is nose-diving. Well, I'm hoping to get some tips from the conference I'm attending tomorrow up in Manchester on 'Stretching your brand muscles'. I'm taking Hugo's place as he thought he should be giving the talk, not listening to other lesser brand beings lecturing him. He was also not worried about missing out on the pre-conference corporate jolly at Old Trafford to watch England play Poland at football. Apparently Hugo prefers his balls to be oval-shaped, not round.

HUGO'S NEW CLOTHES (WEDNESDAY, MARCH 7)

The England game held no surprises. A mediocre match with our star striker sent off in front of his home crowd, and a spectacularly stupid blunder from our goal-keeper gifting Poland a 1–0 victory. More surprising was today's branding conference. I had expected it to be packed full of PowerPoint-powered pontification, but instead the day was made up of practical case studies. As my year as a CROFTer progresses, I am increasingly feeling like the little boy in the story of the Emperor's New Clothes. In my case, it is Hugo who is stark naked, convinced the latest brand thinking is dressing him for success. He's clearly a clever bloke, but it seems to me he's been seduced by some dodgy theories about how to build a brand.

The first case study of the day was on the Dove brand, and specifically about their cleansing bar business. Everything I had read about Dove focused on their 'Campaign for Real Beauty' and the advert for their firming creams with the full-figured ladies in their white underwear. They'd even made a five-minute appearance on the Oprah Winfrey Show. Well, it turns out that although the Dove brand has been stretched into new categories such as the firming range, deodorant and shampoos, the biggest and most profitable bit of their sales still comes from the original bar with '1/4 moisturizing cream'. Most of the new products also have the same 1/4 moisturizing cream content, creating a unique and consistent link between them. What was really impressive was the way they have been able to grow the market share of the bar in the USA, even though many people in the company thought this was a mature market with nowhere to go but down (sounds familiar). The recipe for this success seemed to have a few key elements:

- They kept advertising the bar – with any new product launches getting extra support, not stealing from it.

- They worked on improvements to the original white bar, and created new versions such as a refreshing green one.
- A direct marketing campaign to 300 000 'bar fans' was used to strengthen their attachment to the brand.

The Dove brand manager summed this up by saying that the team 'loved the bar' (wheresthesausage.com) and recognized that brand stretching was only possible because this original bit of the business was strong and healthy. What a contrast to Simpton's. I didn't see a whole lot of sausage love going on. Advertising had been axed to fund the pizza launch. We had been cutting corners, not creating core innovation. And we were chasing after elusive younger consumers and ignoring our loyal fans, assuming we had any left.

But the best bit of the day was a presentation by a professor from the North of England Business School in Rotherham. He showed how most brand extension was an exercise in what he called 'brand ego tripping', where brands get too big for their boots and stretch into markets where they don't belong. The audience laughed when he showed 'The extension graveyard' (Figure 3.1), made up of real-life products that had died early and well-deserved deaths, such as Cosmopolitan yoghurt, Bic perfume and Levi's formal suits. I was the only one who didn't laugh, as I could already see a fresh, pizza box-shaped hole being dug in the ground. The main case study was on the **easyGroup and their plethora of questionable extensions** (wheresthesausage.com).

It seems that easyGroup's first and by far most successful launch was easyJet, based on a simple but highly effective winning formula. First, find a market that is price-sensitive. Create a 'no frills' offer (e.g., no free drinks) and get customers to do some of the work (e.g., booking online). Cut the price to attract

Figure 3.1: The brand extension graveyard

loads of new punters. And use clever pricing (book early, pay less) to get more bums on seats. It's easy to see how this same formula could work for easyGroup's hire cars and even cruises. In these cases the extensions had 'brand added value': different and relevant benefits compared to the stuff currently on offer in the market. However, we all agreed it was much harder to figure out how it applies to pizza delivery (we do the ingredients, you make your own pizza) or watches (what, you want hands on your watch?).

The lessons were clear. The further you stretch away from what made you famous, the harder it is to pull this off without your brand elastic snapping. And when you do extend, it's best to have some link back to what made you famous in the first place, like Dove's 1/4 moisturizing cream.

Took the chance to pop into the factory on the way to Old Trafford. Ron was almost more surprised to see me this time; I guess he thought my previous visit had been a one-off as part of my induction process. I discussed with him the findings from my informal sausage sampling, and in particular what it would cost to go back to the 'original' recipe. He promised to do a proper calculation, but off the top of his head thought we were talking about an extra 20–30p a pack.

SPRAY MORE, GET MORE (TUESDAY, MARCH 13)

Popped into Boots at lunchtime to look for a birthday present for my nephew Techno Tim. Came across a boxed set of Lynx body spray and decided it was worth one last attempt to work on his personal hygiene. Chances are he will keep the deck of playing cards adorned with half-naked ladies from the Lynx advertising and leave the body spray languishing in his bathroom cupboard, if he has such a thing. However, the money I spent was not completely wasted, as it gave me another useful tip. The Lynx pack reminded me of the advert I had seen the week before that ended with the line 'Spray more, get more'. The idea was that by spraying all over your body, not just under your arms, you had a better chance of bedding the babe of your dreams. It seemed that as with the Dove brand, **Lynx was looking for ways to grow by increasing use of their main product** (wheresthesausage.com). The ad showed a guy spraying Lynx on a coat-stand, with his girl-friend responding by lap-dancing around it. He then sprays the can from his neck all the way down to his waistline and waits for the girl to follow the same path. I went back to the shelf and put an extra pack in my basket to try out with Claire tonight. After all, I seem to remember reading in one of her magazines an article about how trendy pole dancing was as a fitness regime.

A MAN WITH A PLAN (TUESDAY, MARCH 20)

I booked a meeting room to get some peace and quiet, and wrote my first ever full-blown brand presentation, making the case for stopping the pizza train and re-launching our core sausage business instead. When I proudly shared my work with Jane her eyes grew as big as a pair of our pizzas and she wailed that I'd written a suicide note. As she sees it, 'the pizza train has left the station' and there's no turning back. She has got a point. My old colleagues in sales presented the pizza launch to the supermarkets months ago, and booked in pro-motions and launch support. The sales figures for the pizza were in our 2007 plan, and without the 'pipeline' fill Jane ex-plained to me before, we hadn't a hope in hell of hitting our targets. Reluctantly, I agreed to sleep on it rather than rushing in to see Hugo with my plan.

Told Claire about my anti-pizza plan over dinner, but she wasn't exactly 'on the same page as me'. In fact, she wasn't reading the same book, or even sitting in the same library. She reminded me that we still had a mountain of a mortgage to pay each month, not to mention the viciously expensive fees for Amy's new private school. If Hugo wanted to launch a pizza, then I should back him up 100%. If she had her way I think I'd be off to Tuscany to stick the olives on myself.

Whilst I was disappointed that Claire had not been more impressed by my fledgling brand strategy skills, she did have a point. It was one thing to *think* that Hugo's brand strategy was fatally flawed. It was another thing to write a presentation that rammed this down his throat.

I went off to the study for a sulk and came up with a compromise plan that involved me looking at plans to grow the core sausage business, whilst steaming ahead Titanic-like with the pizza launch. After all, Jane was doing most of the actual work on the pizza, and had things under control. Decided to delay my Lynx pole-dancing experiment till another night when Claire was in a better mood.

OFF AND RUNNING (THURSDAY, MARCH 22)

Caught Hugo on a good day, as he had just found out that he was up from 87 to 65 in *Marketing* magazine's hot 100 marketing movers and shakers. He was especially pleased that they'd used the new photo he had commissioned, which showed him standing at the top of the stairwell in the office looking down moodily with a furrowed brow. He reluctantly agreed with my plan, as long as it didn't involve spending any money and I did the work in addition to launching the pizza. The clincher was my suggestion that by letting me work on the sausage business he didn't need a new brand manager to fill the vacant job on the core business, leaving more cash for the pizza launch.

This was a good way to end my first quarter as a brand management CROFTer, and I no longer feel like going back to my old boss in Sales on my hands and knees, begging for my old job back. I am determined to give this branding thing my best shot. I'm also starting to learn a whole new language that I've called 'Hugo-speak'. Here are a few examples:

Hugo-speak	English
Leverage our brand equities to extend into new market categories	Launch a new pizza
Connect with consumers at a higher level to create life-long loyalty	Make people like us so they buy more
Go beyond the purely functional product to promise an emotional experience	As the product's crap, add some spin
Refresh our brand identity and re-brand	Change our logo

MARCH'S SUMMARY

1. You need a strong and growing core business before you think about stretching.
2. Stretch your brand elastic too far and it will snap.
3. Many brand extensions are 'brand ego trips', offering nothing new compared with what is already on offer.
4. My own definition of brand management is 'common sense, made complicated'.

Quarter Two

FROM INSIGHT TO BRAND VISION

4.

April – Be the consumer (don't over-rely on research)

DO NOT DISTURB: ARTIST AT WORK (TUESDAY, APRIL 3)

This morning I decided to test out Hugo's 'open-door' policy with a question about the rationale for going after young urban consumers not families. I found his door firmly closed and waited outside for 15 minutes, during which time Hugo was engrossed in a heated phone conversation. Even with the door closed I could hear him screaming McEnroe-like that he simply could not believe it. I wondered if the latest monthly market share results were the subject of his anger, as they didn't make pretty reading; we'd lost another share point, making it 20 consecutive months of decline.

I knocked on the door and popped my head tentatively around, summoning up my best brand-speak to ask Hugo if I could 'bounce an idea' off him. He motioned for me to enter as he marched up and down in disgust. Seeking to show solidarity, I suggested optimistically that our market share had perhaps hit the bottom. Hugo stopped pacing, frowned and looked at me with a confused expression. Seems that share results were the last thing on his mind. His anger was caused by ETC only getting upper circle tickets for the Royal Opera House performance of La Bohème, not the stall seats he was used to. Our conversation continued in the artistic vein when I voiced my concerns about how interested young urban consumers would be in our brand. Hugo replied that Picasso didn't ask people what they wanted before painting his next masterpiece; he created and the adoring public followed. And the same thing would happen with the Simpton's 'brand renaissance'. He suggested that if I wanted to discuss something as mundane as consumers, then I should take it up with Jane.

When I asked Jane about our consumer target, she picked the brand pyramid off the wall and read out what was written with the same enthusiasm as Amy practising her 12 times tables. When I complained that I was having problems understanding who this consumer really was, Jane perked up and said that she did have a solution. She had organized some focus groups later in the week to explore concepts for our new pizza, and I was welcome to come along. On the question about whether our current customers weren't families, Jane said she'd ask Brian to get some data for us.

THE MAN IN THE MIRROR (THURSDAY, APRIL 5)

Spent this evening sitting through the focus groups, and it was certainly an eventful affair. It also saved me from a night out with the pushy parents from Amy's class at school. It's one thing to nod a polite hello to them in the playground, it's another thing altogether to listen to them droning on and on about how proud they are that their precious little offspring speaks fluent Japanese, rides a pony bare-back and prefers Shakespeare to the Simpson's.

The venue for the research was conveniently located close to the Royal Opera House, where Hugo and the ETC team headed off just as the first group was starting. This left Jane, Brian and myself sitting behind the one-way mirror that allowed us to see the eight ladies sat in a circle eating soggy sandwiches, without them seeing us. The mirror was so convincing that one of the ladies came right up close to look in it and adjust her hairstyle.

After the focus group participants had helped themselves to an extra large glass of free wine, Susy the 'moderator' who was running the session kicked things off. She asked everyone to say what sort of animal they would like to be, in an attempt to break the ice. However, the exercise clearly left the participants bemused, being something of a mental double-somersault with a back-flip when most of them looked barely capable of a lazy forward roll. Susy took the hint and moved the conversation onto sausages.

I know the ladies were all getting paid £30 for their trouble, but boy did they earn it. Susy was asking them to remember in vivid detail their last sausage-cooking experience, which for some of them was a few weeks ago. She reminded me of an irritatingly inquisitive toddler in the way she responded to every answer with 'why?'. I thought at one point she was going to grab the table lamp and shine it in the eyes of one of the less responsive ladies to cajole her into baring more of her soul. It all seemed rather artificial and forced. I asked Jane what she could remember about her last sausage-cooking experience, at which point she reddened with embarrassment and tried to divert my attention by offering me another cold beer. I accepted the beer, but didn't let Jane off the hook. She owned up that she never ate sausages. Ever. I had a horrible feeling she wasn't the only one on the team like this, and I pointed with my beer bottle towards Brian. Jane shook her head and mouthed the word 'veggie'. It turns out the one team member who *did* eat the occasional sausage was Hugo. Jane told me he was rather fond of the bangers and mash served at his favourite upmarket eatery, the Ivy.

Susy had worked her way through the first part of her interrogation, sorry questionnaire, made up of general questions about buying and cooking sausages. She proudly summarized the 20-step process that they had come up with together. Could it really be that complicated, I wondered? Jane enthusiastically noted down all 20 steps in the form of little interconnected bubbles, so she obviously found it useful. But I had the impression that the people there had come up with such a complex process because they had been asked to, and they wanted to please Susy.

It was then time to get onto the main subject of the evening: concepts for the new pizza range. Jane handed me a stapled set of ten A4 pages, each with several dense paragraphs of text. After reading the first three of these I was confused, and I worked on the brand team. They were very dry, complicated and all seemed to be very similar. The ladies in the group seemed to agree with me, and on seeing the second board one of them complained that she didn't like 'the advert'. Susy turned slowly to face her, her jaws clenched together so hard that little dimples appeared in her cheeks. She explained through gritted teeth that these were *not* adverts, they were *concepts*. I knew what the poor lady was going to reply, and felt like one of those bodyguards who throw themselves in the line of fire when someone tries to shoot the President of the United States. But I was too late. She asked in a whisper the question on the lips of the other seven ladies: *'What's a concept?'* Susy threw down the board in disgust and stormed out of the room in a huff, saying that she couldn't work with this sort of consumer.

SEEING CONSUMERS IN 3-D (TUESDAY, APRIL 10)

Went into London for a meeting with INK to discuss the ramifications of the focus group debacle on the pizza packaging. After the meeting finished I headed over to the City to meet my mate Tom at Fresh Italy, the chain of shops he runs that sell fresh, fast Italian food. Fresh pasta, risotto and the like, all cooked in front of you by chefs. I also got three new ideas about what this consumer insight thing was all about.

By the time I got there at 1pm the place was heaving with the lunchtime rush hour. Tom was busy talking to one of his team, so I joined the queue and looked up at the menu to pick what I would have. As I got to the front a young woman walked straight past me, grabbed a bag that was sitting on the counter and strode off without paying. I was about to run after the woman and demand she pay, when Tom came up to the counter to serve me. When I told him about the lady who had done a runner, he laughed and told me not to worry.

It turns out that the customer in question was using Tom's **new service allowing people to order their lunch from their computer whilst at work** (wheresthesausage.com). The kitchen got cooking and told the customer when to come and pick up the food. When you log in, they even tell you what you ate last time and ask you if you want the same again, which it turns out most people do. You save precious time by not having to queue, and don't have to worry about carrying cash as the food is charged to your credit card.

I quizzed Tom about where the idea for the service came from, and if he had used focus groups. The idea had actually come from a much simpler, cheaper source, which it seems to me is also much more effective: observing customers and chatting to them as they queued up for their food.

The second thing I learnt about was how to describe your consumer. The Fresh Italy team had painted a colourful 'portrait' of their target customer, who they christened 'Rachel'. Tom took a folded-up photo of Rachel out of his wallet and turned it over. On the back he had drawn four boxes that answered questions about her, such as her hobbies and what she needed from lunchtime food. From reading the profile, I got a good picture of the sort of person Fresh Italy was aiming at. With such a vivid picture of the target customer, the team came up with loads of ideas for new services, including the PC ordering one. Rachel's lunchtime was precious, and 10 minutes less time in the queue meant 10 more minutes for chatting with her mates or checking out the latest gossip in *Heat*.

The final thing I learnt about was exploring new ideas. With the PC ordering system, they didn't write out wordy concepts like the ones for our pizzas. Instead, they got a prototype web-site mocked up, and then asked some of their loyal customers to try it out for real. It was much easier for them to get the idea by seeing what it would really look like, rather than reading it on a sheet of paper.

My concern with Tom's approach was that by focusing on people like Rachel, wasn't he missing out on other potential user groups such as families or tourists. His reply was that you needed to be clear on who was your *main* target and build the brand mainly for them. There would then be some secondary targets, who have the same needs and attitudes on certain occasions (Figure 4.1). Thinking about it reminded me of the old saying, 'try and appeal to everyone and you'll appeal to no-one'. And this is exactly what we were trying to do in the target audience of our brand pyramid.

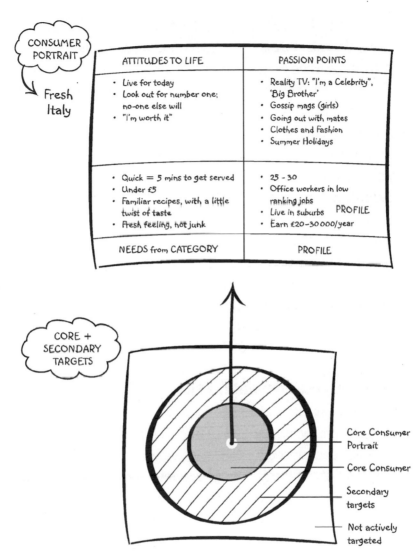

CONSUMER PORTRAIT

Fresh Italy

ATTITUDES TO LIFE	PASSION POINTS
• Live for today • Look out for number one; no-one else will • "I'm worth it"	• Reality TV: "I'm a Celebrity", 'Big Brother' • Gossip mags (girls) • Going out with mates • Clothes and Fashion • Summer Holidays
• Quick = 5 mins to get served • Under £5 • Familiar recipes, with a little twist of taste • Fresh feeling, not junk	• 25 - 30 • Office workers in low ranking jobs • Live in suburbs PROFILE • Earn £20-30 000/year
NEEDS from CATEGORY	PROFILE

CORE + SECONDARY TARGETS

Core Consumer Portrait

Core Consumer

Secondary targets

Not actively targeted

Figure 4.1: Core consumer portrait

FOLLOW THE MONEY (FRIDAY, APRIL 13)

Brian came to see me with the data on our consumers today. He really was a whizz with numbers, and had done a range of helpful graphs. As I had guessed, it turns out that by far our biggest source of business is families with kids. They're about 30% of the

UK population, but a whopping 65% of our sales. Thinking about my own life so far helped me understand these figures. I ate the odd sausage when I was a student, but most of these came with chips and gravy from the local take-away. When I got my first job, I bought lots of ready meals as I had neither the time nor the inclination to cook. However, when I met Claire and we settled down and had kids, I rediscovered the desire for a Sunday morning fry-up. The other thing the data backed up was a seasonal peak during the summer months, when the barbeque season got into swing. This was a habit that had really caught on in the UK, though it was still not as big as in the USA.

It seemed to me that by chasing after younger, urban and more affluent consumers we were leaving behind our heartland of families with kids. Wouldn't we be better off 'following the money' and trying to get more of these people, or persuade existing customers to buy us more often?

BE THE CONSUMER (MONDAY, APRIL 16)

I got another injection of inspiration about consumer insight on Saturday night, when we had dinner with a friend called Anna who does headhunting for Nike. I was talking to her about what I had learnt about the limits of research, and she told me the most interesting thing. Nike don't do any conventional research at all. None. They can do this because **they only hire people who love sport and are actively involved in at least one** (wheresthesausage.com). Anna looked down rather disapprovingly at my ever-expanding waistline as she explained this. I guess drinking a whole six-pack of beer whilst watching the Six Nations rugby tournament doesn't count. Nike's recruitment policy meant that their team was full of people who were not trying to understand the consumer. They *were* the consumer. They had an intuitive sense of what would work or not work for

Nike, that they felt in their guts. Their insight was not just rational, it was emotional.

I thought back to the conversation with Jane about our team, and the contrast was stark. Never mind being avid fans of our product, they didn't use it at all. Their lives were miles away from our core family users. As a result, they used research like a drunk uses a lamp-post: for support, not illumination. I decided a quick and easy way to immerse Brian and Jane in the consumer world was to invite them over for one of my fry-ups next weekend.

BRAND BOND (WEDNESDAY, APRIL 18)

Great night out to see Casino Royale, the new James Bond film. Claire and I talked about the movie over dinner and both agreed that the producers had done a very clever job at updating the Bond 'brand', if you can call it that. We played a silly game to see how many features and catchphrases they had managed to stay loyal to over the years, and came up with at least 20. These included:

- The basic idea: 'Bond vs. the baddie to save the world'.
- The theme tune.
- The gadgets.
- Characters: 'M' (James Bond's boss), Miss Moneypenny.
- Cars.
- Girls, girls, girls.
- 'Bond, James Bond'.
- 'Martini, shaken not stirred'.

But whilst a lot of elements stayed the same, **the producers also managed to update the brand to keep it relevant for today** (wheresthesausage.com). And they really needed to do this when you think how much the world has changed in the last 20 years. Firstly, the world is a lot more dangerous and complex. Gone are the days of the Cold War; welcome to the era of global terrorism. Also, the baddies have got badder. Looking back at Dr No, he seems like a real gent compared with the evil foes Bond now has to face. The competitive environment around James Bond is also a lot tougher now. There are other spy films to compete with, such as the Bourne Supremacy. But there are also competitive entertainment brands in other channels, such as the 24 series on television, and the rise of video games.

I scribbled a drawing on the cinema magazine I picked up so I would remember our discussion and see if it had any relevance to product brands at Simpton's (Figure 4.2). I thought it would do, as one of my concerns with our brand strategy is the way we seem to be forgetting what made us famous.

THE STELLA TEST (MONDAY, APRIL 23)

It looks like my brand Bond theory of sticking to what made you famous may also apply to consumer products closer to home. I was reading the *Times* magazine at lunch today when I saw an advert for the beer brand Stella Artois. It reminded me of the brilliant TV adverts they'd been running for ages. When I thought about them, I had the impression that they had been pretty consistent over the years, much like James Bond. I wanted to get hold of the Stella advertising quickly so I could check out my new theory, and asked Brian if he had any ideas. He told me to give him a few minutes.

Ten minutes later he beckoned me over to his desk with a grin of satisfaction on his face, pointing to the screen of his PC. I could see that we were on a page of the You Tube website, and he had compiled together on one page

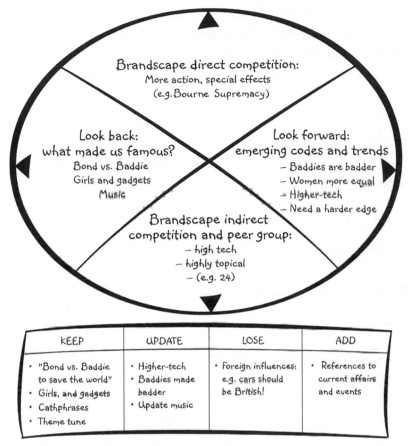

Figure 4.2: Remember what made you famous

a selection of Stella Artois adverts from the last 20 years. He stood up and offered me a place in his chair so I could check out his handiwork. Clicking on each video I was able to watch the brand's history unfold before me. And in doing so I confirmed that **Stella had also been very clever about identifying a number of key brand elements and sticking to them over the years** (wheresthesausage.com). The story was basically the same: 'You'd give anything for a Stella'. My favourite featured a flower seller who gives the bar owner a single rose in return for a sandwich, only to see another customer order a glass of Stella that suddenly makes him very thirsty. He offers the inn keeper one rose, then two, then three, but to no avail. Eventually we seem him savouring his beer and pan back to see the entire bar covered in roses.

In addition to sticking to the same story, several other things came back again and again:

- The music.
- All the dialogue in French (quite something for a brand targeting beer-swilling blokes).
- Beautifully filmed, long 60-second adverts.
- The 'Reassuringly expensive' line.

I congratulated Brian on his handiwork, and asked if he could do the same advertising history for Simpton's. After he'd stopped laughing, he explained that videos were uploaded to YouTube because people thought they were funny or cool and he doubted that anyone was sad enough to think this about a Simpton's sausages ad. I typed in the brand name anyway, but Brian's doubts were confirmed when the search came up empty.

Later, I asked Jane if she had a compilation of Simpton's advertising so I could do the 'Stella test' on them, but she looked at me as if I'd asked for the Holy Grail. She explained that she had only been on the brand for 12 months, and anything before that was ancient history to her. She suggested the one person who might have such a thing would be Old Mr Simpton.

SUPERMARKET SCHUMACHER (SATURDAY, APRIL 28)

The weekend got off to a bad start this morning when we were woken by the postman ringing the bell at 7.30am, on one of the rare occasions the kids had slept late. Claire stormed downstairs threatening me with divorce if it was one of my Amazon deliveries, which fortunately it wasn't. It was a cold-box filled with sausages from the Simpton's factory that Ron had worked up for me, using the original, pre-Hugo recipe. This reminded me that I needed to stook up for tomorrow's team fry-up, when I had invited Jane and Brian to come over and sample our stuff against a range of competitive brands.

Got into more trouble when I lost track of time in the supermarket and ended up spending over an hour in front of Sainsbury's sausage section. When I realized how late I was, I sped round the supermarket like Michael Schumacher, with his trademark disrespect for other drivers' safety causing a hail of angry insults as I bumped people out of the way. In my haste I bought normal ketchup, not organic, and forgot a host of other essential items from Claire's list.

Well, at least the time spent was useful. The first thing that struck me is how little time people spent choosing. I remembered back to the 20-step process from the focus group. A few minutes actually doing some shopping would show her how far from the truth it really was. All the people I saw scanned the shelf briefly, zoomed in on a pack that caught their attention like a heat-seeking missile and then 'bang!', their hand shot out and grabbed it. I plucked up the courage to ask a few people to explain their purchases, and the initial embarrassment was worth it for the learning I got. Most people simply said they always bought the same sausages week in, week out. They had a favourite brand, in most cases Sainsbury's Taste the

Difference, and they stuck to it. A couple of people said they were attracted by the fancy packaging of Royal Duchy sausages, but sheepishly put them back on the shelf when I pointed out how expensive they were. And not one of the ten or so shoppers I saw bothered to bend down and pick up a pack of Simpton's. When I pointed out our packs languishing low down on the shelf most people said they had not even seen them, and never considered them any more. We were something they had bought in the past, but that had somehow just faded into obscurity. The other comment people made was how outdated and cheap our packaging looked compared with Sainsbury's. They were all shocked to hear that we charged the same price, expecting us to be cheaper. Ow.

ALL FRIED UP (MONDAY, APRIL 30)

The Sunday fry-up was a lot of fun, if a rather depressing confirmation of how far our product quality has fallen behind since Old Mr Simpton handed over the reins of the business to his nephew. Jane and Brian did turn up, against my expectations, although they didn't eat much as they were both suffering from Olympic hangovers. The old recipe Simpton's sausages got the thumbs up from Claire and the kids, with a nice firm texture and rich taste that they summed up as 'traditional, not fancy. The way a sausage should be'. You could also see by just grilling them that they had less fat compared with the new ones we were now selling, which when pricked spurted out grease like some gunk-spewing monster in a cheap horror movie. The Sainsbury's Taste the Difference ones were best of the bunch, and also won the vote for the best packaging. Whilst ours had a list of e-numbers that sounded like the recipe for a chemical weapon, not a sausage, the Sainsbury's ones were all natural. They were also organic, and had a nice story about the farmer who made them. But at least there was some hope, as the original Simpton's sausages came a close second. I took a photo of us all enjoying Ron's handiwork, and emailed it to him and the team at the factory.

I also made some notes about our target consumer profile, along the lines of the format Tom had shown me (Figure 4.3). This re-focused us firmly back on Mums (or Dads) buying sausages for their family, and not the younger trend-setters that Hugo wanted to chase after. Being a consumer myself helped to write this profile, and I had also found some interesting findings hidden in some old research documents. I had a go at what the key insight was we could tap into, using some tips from a really interesting case study on the Pampers brand I'd read about on a branding website. I liked the definition it gave of an insight as 'A discovery about your consumer that opens the door to an opportunity for your brand'. The trick was getting beyond observations of consumer behaviour to the deeper emotions people feel. For Pampers, this was that 'Babies with healthy skin are happier... and so better able to play, learn and develop'.

The finding that babies are happier when they have healthy skin rather than nappy rash was not that new. The true insight came from talking to researchers into child behaviour who explained that by being dry and getting a good night's sleep babies were better able to play, and that this in turn was key to their development. **It was this insight that led to a brand vision about 'Celebrating baby development' and being with parents to help them in this every step of the way** (wheresthesausage.com).

When I thought about our brand, the finding was about the importance of good food that was natural, authentic and not

ATTITUDES TO LIFE	PASSTIMES
• Juggling different things (job, family, self) • Family and kids are the most important thing • Cooking is something she likes, though doesn't always have time	• Reading a mixture of quality papers, and more trashy gossip magazines • Ski and summer holidays • Walks in the country • Tries to go swimming when she can

WHO ARE WE TALKING TO?

• Likes natural food, with no nasties • Takes more care now she is feeding the kids, so ready to pay a bit more for good quality • Likes variety to keep the kids interested in eating	• Mum aged 35-40, with 2 kids aged 5 and 8 • Working part-time • Pretty well-off, lives in a nice suburb of a big city
WHAT they WANT	PROFILE

Figure 4.3: Core consumer portrait for Simpton's

full of artificial ingredients. But what was the deeper insight we could tap into? My gut feeling was that this was something to do with the power of good grub like ours to bring the family back together round the table, something I knew happened less and less often in today's busy world.

APRIL'S SUMMARY

1. True insight doesn't come from focus groups, it comes from immersing yourself in your consumers' world.

2. This is a whole lot easier if you *are* the consumer, or at least use the product.

3. By having a tight consumer target, you can create a colourful portrait of them and their life.

4. Keeping a brand healthy requires a balancing act: remembering what made you famous, whilst looking ahead to new trends.

5.

May – GPS for your brand (creating a clear vision to keep you on track)

HUGO'S HARLEY? (WEDNESDAY, MAY 2)

I want to start working on the direction for our brand, as today's 'jam session' with Hugo reinforced my feeling that his vision for Simpton's is dangerously flawed. At least I now understand where he's been getting his ideas from. He has been seduced by a new brand bandwagon that he wants us all to jump on, called 'Hugbrands'. According to this theory, it's no longer enough to be liked by our consumers, we have to be loved and hugged tightly to their chests. Loyalty was out of the window (not that we had a lot to chuck out), replaced by devotion. He spoke with a fervour that reminded me of the Gospel Vicar played by James Brown in the Blues Brothers movie.

Hugo waxed lyrical about how Prada, Absolut and Nike were not just products or brands, but icons of modern culture. But he saved his most breathless moment of adoration for Harley Davidson, and showed us a brand movie Tim had found for him on You Tube. It talked about the brand's beliefs and philosophy, such as fighting back against a society that wanted to 'smash individuals like bugs on a windscreen'.

When Hugo asked us to start jamming I, of course, made another one of my career-limiting comments. I said that sausages seemed to be a long way from the 'lifestyle brands' he had shown us. Weren't we closer to pasta sauce than Prada, I asked? Hugo stood up abruptly and picked up a huge board. He slowly raised it above his head, as if he was offering up to the Hugmarks gods in worship. Then, with a flourish, he revealed a poster of what looked like a bare-backed Harley Davidson rider. On his back was a huge tattoo, but not the one you'd expect. In place of the Harley logo was… the Simpton's brand, illustrating how strong a bond our users, or rather hugsters, would have with us. I had a sneaking suspicion that the local tattoo parlour would not be over-run with bikers asking for the Simpton's logo in place of the Harley eagle, but kept this to myself.

I decided to do some homework on the Harley Davidson brand and Tim helped me track down the You Tube film. On watching it, two things struck me. Firstly, in a category like ours surely we needed more sausage (product) and less sizzle (emotion) than a lifestyle brand like Harley Davidson. Their fans would go as far as wearing a Harley jacket or having the brand tattooed on them because the brand was a 'badge' they wore to say something about themselves to the world. Our brand's emotion was more about what it made you feel like inside, and the product itself was much more important. The second, and perhaps more surprising, thing was **the starring role played by the Harley Davidson product** (wheresthesausage.com). I scribbled down some of the product features they believed in:

- 'Rumbling engines'
- 'Pistons the size of garbage cans'

- 'Fuel tanks designed in 1936'
- 'Freight train-sized headlights'
- 'Chrome and custom paint'

So, even for a lifestyle brand like Harley, the foundation of the brand was a fantastic, differentiated product. And as long as we lacked a decent sausage, no amount of Simpsational sizzle was going to save us.

BREAKING OUT OF THE BOXES (FRIDAY, MAY 4)

Inspired by the Harley Davidson brand video, I dug out the brand pyramid that had been presented at the Babbington House workshop. Not quite as motivating as a vision for our brand, to say the least. Granted, we were never going to be any-where near as sexy as Harley Davidson, apart from in Hugo's dreams. But surely we could do better than this thing? For a start it was so complicated and full of words and had so many boxes. It was also hard to know where to start and how to climb up it. And most importantly of course, the fundamental idea about becoming a lifestyle brand felt wrong to me.

I was convinced we could do better, but had to be careful not to get sacked by challenging Hugo's pyramid, which was something of a protected monument. Instead, my plan was to do the work as part of my review on the core sausage business. As this was the only bit of the business I thought we should have it was, de facto, my version of the brand vision.

I was stuck on where to start, having never worked on such a thing before, and asked Jane what process had been used to create the current brand vision. She said that ETC had been emailed the blank pyramid by Hugo and asked to 'fill in the boxes', which they duly did, spending weeks to get the words just right. Hugo sent it back several times to be re-worked, before proclaiming it in line with best branding practice. This didn't seem the way to go, as it sounded a very rational and unexciting process. Creating something as inspiring as the Harley video surely didn't come from filling in the boxes on a pyramid.

Inspiration on how to get started came from reading a supplement to *Marketing* magazine with the winners of the Marketing Society's annual awards. The case study that grabbed my attention was on T-Mobile, the mobile phone network. They did lots of work on **bringing to life their consumer and asked a series of challenging questions about where they wanted to go with their brand** (wheresthesausage.com). They then explored their ideas with consumers and people in the business, before finalizing the strategy and working on an action plan. I especially liked this last bit, as it sounded practical and business-focused.

We had a pretty good start with the target consumer part, with the profile I had done that re-focused us back on Mums with young kids. We had also defined the insight around cooking good food being not just about filling stomachs, but about bringing the family together around the table as a 'family circle'. What we needed to do now was work on where to go with our brand. I picked out one exercise as a good place to get started, which was called the 'brand manifesto'. This involved imagining that we were going to march in the street and carry a banner protesting about something we really cared about. In the case of T-Mobile this was to do with all the techno-speak and sneaky pricing used to bamboozle people. I decided to set up a working lunch with the team to do this for Simpton's sausages, and sent out an email straight away.

MARCHING IN THE STREET (WEDNESDAY, MAY 9)

Brian, Jane and I spent lunch today working on the brand manifesto, along with a mate from Sales called John who I dragged in screaming and kicking. Even he enjoyed it in the end, although this may have been something to do with the free sausage sandwiches and mugs of coffee. And we came up with some stuff that was a damn site better than the Simpsational pyramid we're stuck with at the moment.

I used a series of questions to stimulate the thinking, which I'd picked out of the T-Mobile case study:

- What did we believe in?
- What were we proud of?
- What did we fight against, what pissed us off?
- What did we fight for?

I gave everyone a big flag drawn on flipchart paper and asked them to scrawl on it with a marker pen. It took a while to get people in the mood, and there were of course a few less than serious statements at the start. But after a while we got into it, and for the first time since I'd been on the brand I felt we were expressing some genuine feelings about the brand. Jane's flag in particular struck me as really interesting. It turns out the Sunday morning tasting session at my house had really touched her, something I had not picked up on at the time. She was a Northern girl who had been attracted by the bright lights of London (or Surrey to be more accurate), and felt obliged to cut off her roots with home. She was trying to live what she thought was the City girl lifestyle of restaurants, pubs and clubs but deep down missed the comforts of home. The Sunday sausage session reminded her of times when her own Dad would do a traditional fry-up, and she somehow felt like she was 'back home'. Other flags picked up on similar themes, talking about the world being too fast, high-tech, complicated and fragmented. People didn't eat together any more. Brian came up with some useful trivia he had found on Google: only 30% of families ate together regularly, and an amazing 20% didn't even have a table to eat on!

Another theme that came through our work was the obsession with health. Of course we all agreed that obesity was a real problem, but the solution was all to do with balance – eating the right mix of foods and getting plenty of exercise. Sausages were a treat to enjoy once or twice a week, not every day.

And when I pushed people on what made us angry, we all expressed frustration at the way we had let own label brands steal our shirt, through a lack of innovation. It was John who reminded us that we had a proud heritage going back over 200 years when George Simpton started the business. We had walked away from his founding principles by cutting quality, not improving it.

Everyone was impressed by how much we had got through in just a couple of hours. I volunteered to type up our flags and do a summary, and everyone agreed to meet in a week's time to review the results and do some more work on the brand (Figure 5.1).

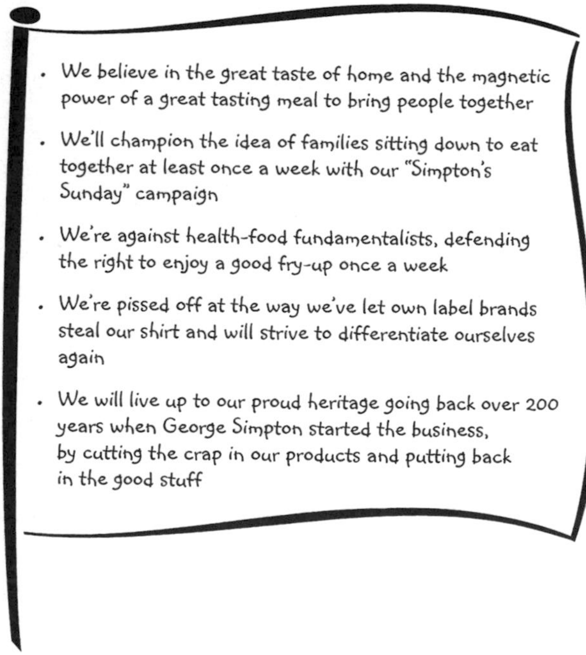

- We believe in the great taste of home and the magnetic power of a great tasting meal to bring people together

- We'll champion the idea of families sitting down to eat together at least once a week with our "Simpton's Sunday" campaign

- We're against health-food fundamentalists, defending the right to enjoy a good fry-up once a week

- We're pissed off at the way we've let own label brands steal our shirt and will strive to differentiate ourselves again

- We will live up to our proud heritage going back over 200 years when George Simpton started the business, by cutting the crap in our products and putting back in the good stuff

Figure 5.1: Brand Manifesto for Simpton's

BLAST FROM THE PAST (MONDAY, MAY 14)

In this morning's post I got a blast from the past. It was an advertising reel from Ron, which he'd been good enough to have transferred from VHS to DVD. I invited Brian and Jane to huddle round my PC and we watched it together. The first adverts were so old they were in black and white, and were painfully outdated. They showed Mum hard at work in the kitchen with a blonde-haired daughter, whilst Dad toiled over an oily car with his son. The commercial ended with the slogan: 'The best British banger, bar none'. What struck us as we watched the next few adverts from the 1960s and 1970s was how the same basic idea had been maintained – hard work paying off with the reward of a Simpton's sausage lunch. And the endline remained the same.

In the 1980s and 1990s the campaign changed, with the introduction of a family that lasted a full 15 years; our very own Stella Artois campaign! Each commercial showed a little bit of their life, almost like a mini soap opera. In each case there was some form of separation, or dispute, with Simpton's part of the solution to bring the family back together again. I actually had to hand Jane my hankie during the one with a teen-age daughter going off to college and failing to call home to talk to her worried parents. The absent daughter finally returns for the holidays, and after enjoying a Simpton's Sunday fry-up she looks up and says simply 'Thanks Mum'. This campaign also had a consistent endline, which I made a note of: 'There's no taste like home'. Then, as we entered the new millennium, the campaign suddenly stopped. I now remembered having read a newspaper article about the 'retirement' of the family, which had resulted in hundreds of people actually protesting. But this was to no avail. The new management, led by Old Mr Simpton's nephew, had instigated a ruthless cost-cutting exercise and taken the brand off air. And then silence. It was as if the Simpton's story had come to an end. The black screen at the end was a fitting symbol for the fortunes of our brand.

COMPLETING THE RECIPE (FRIDAY, MAY 18)

Today we had our second lunchtime brand vision session, and all felt like we were working for some sort of underground brand resistance movement. Brian suggested we even black out our faces and wear camouflage vests, having clearly played one too many video games for his own good. But it was nice to see how he was coming out of his shell more. I shared the final version of the brand manifesto with the team and was pleasantly surprised when they responded with a round of applause. It seemed that this was a much more motivating way of communicating what we stood for than a list of 'brand values'.

This gave me the confidence to carry on with the next set of exercises from the T-Mobile story about our 'nightmare product range'. The idea here was that working on what we didn't want to be was a fun way of working on our vision for the brand. As I watched everyone get stuck in, I knew I'd made the right decision to use these exercises and not just fill in the boxes on a pyramid. I was struck again by the number of common themes that jumped out: products stuffed full of artificial colourings, flavours and preservatives, and only 60% pork. There were also a couple of people brave enough to put up the sausage pizza as well, causing Jane to redden with embarrassment.

We moved on to the next exercise about our nightmare spokesperson for the brand, to work on the 'sizzle': the emotional part of brand. One profile to emerge was that of a second-hand car salesman, conning you into buying an inferior product. Perhaps more interestingly, Jane came up with another type of spokesperson who was a formal food snob, who would only buy their food at Waitrose or Harrods and refused to eat on a table without a tablecloth.

The trick was now to flip these negative visions of our brand into the positive, to get an idea of what we *did* want our brand to stand for. The ideas coming out were both clear and inspiring. For the product side, the key thing was going back to the original Simpton's recipe that had for many years been a guarantee of quality. The recipe had been one of the many things to bite the dust as part of the post-Hugo cost-cutting drive. We'd need Ron's help in putting back pork and taking out artificial rubbish. This product truth should help us convince people they were going to rediscover the great Simpton's taste the whole family loved. This was much easier to understand than the list of unconnected words in the product feature and benefit boxes of Hugo's brand pyramid.

In terms of the emotional sizzle for our brand, Brian proposed the idea of a gastro pub chef who was enthusiastic about introducing great British classics to a younger audience. It would be a guy who refused to cut corners, only accepting the very best ingredients. Although he had been used too much by other companies, and was reaching saturation, we did think of Jamie Oliver as a good example of the sort of personality we wanted for our brand. Importantly, he wasn't a 'health food fundamentalist' who wanted us to all become vegetarians. He loved a good British banger as part of a fry-up every now and then, providing the quality of the produce was right.

Our summary of 'a gastro pub chef... who refuses to cut corners... and has bubbly enthusiasm for great British food' seemed a lot simpler and more vivid than the brand pyramid's list of words in different boxes (personality, values, inner directed emotion, blah, blah).

The final task was to find a way of summing up our idea for the brand. To do this, we thought of slogans to write on our brand team t-shirt. Something snappier than the 'brand essence' we had before, which was 'Accessible aspiration'. We had a few good options, including the simple one of 'The best British banger bar none'. But the one we all picked as the best was 'The real taste of home', which had actually come from looking back at our successful advertising of the past. It was snappy, and worked both in terms of the product and the emotion it helped create of bringing the family back together.

Looking at my watch I was amazed to see it was already 3.00pm; our meeting had run over by half an hour without anyone realizing. How far this work was from the tedious brand pyramid presentation that I had sat through at Babbington House. Rather than a series of boxes full of words, this felt more like we were writing a story for a brand that hung together. It also seemed much more within our grasp, even though a huge amount of work would be needed. I had a very busy day ahead of me with Ron at the factory, that was for sure. As with the last meeting, I agreed to write up the output so we could review it together.

John had the good idea of arranging for the two of us to meet up with a few other people from the sales team to take them through where we'd got to. This would be a good 'torture test' of what we had done, allowing us to get feedback from a non-marketing team who had not been involved with writing the vision. We agreed to fix up a meeting in the pub for a couple of days' time.

BONA FIDE BRAND-MAN (WEDNESDAY, MAY 23)

The presentation to take to the pub test is ready and it's pretty damn hot, if I say so myself. I wrote up the stuff from the two meetings with the team in a PowerPoint presentation, starting with the current pyramid and then going on to reveal our alternative strategy for the brand. I designed a simple format for this which had boxes, but a lot fewer. And you could also find your way through it a lot easier, with a logical flow from the

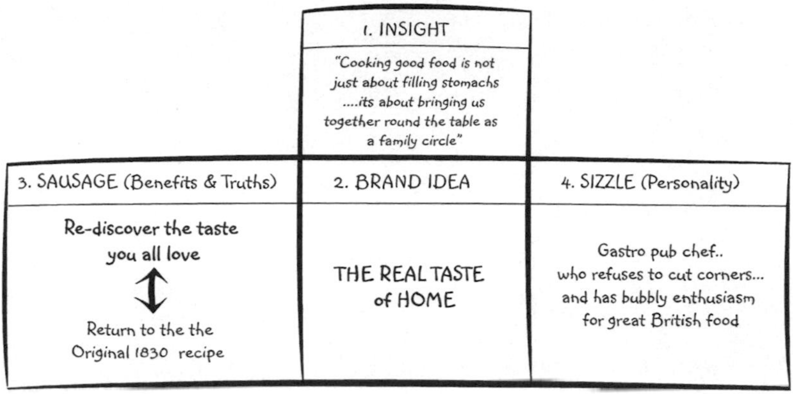

Figure 5.2: Brand Idea for Simpton's

insight to the product/sausage, then the sizzle/emotion and the brand idea (Figure 5.2).

I spent several hours polishing the strategy, and fine-tuning some of the words to get them just right. Brian helped me put in some fancy animation, which I thought was very clever and sure to impress. I finally start to feel like a bona fide brand director.

MAY'S SUMMARY

1. You need to be clear about what sort of brand you are: are you closer to Prada (lifestyle) or pasta sauce (product)?
2. Most great brands are built on a great product, combining sausage and sizzle.
3. Creating a brand vision is not about filling in boxes on some complicated tool. It's about asking yourself some challenging questions about where you want to go and who you want to be.
4. Pick a couple of things you want to deliver (benefits) and make sure for each you have something that supports this (truths).

6.

June – Brand trampoline
(using the brand as a springboard for new ideas)

PUB TEST (TUESDAY, JUNE 5)

Back from the pub test with my tail between my legs. The only bit of light to dispel my gloom is that I know how *not* to use a brand vision.

John had invited two of my old colleagues from Sales to the pub to see the positioning. Mike and Pete both worked in National Accounts, selling to Sainsbury's and Tesco, respectively. He'd also brought along Tessa Williams, who ran Category Development, helping our customers better promote and display the product categories we operated in. She was a feisty Scottish lady who was hotly tipped to be a future Sales Director, and so in direct competition for the job I was hoping to get after my year as a CROFTer. I shot John an evil look as he brought the round of beers back to the table, but he just winked at me.

I took a sip of beer to moisten my throat that was dry with nerves. This was the first time I had ever formally presented a brand strategy. My first wrong move was starting with a re-cap of the Simpsational pyramid. This was met with moans and groans from the table. I knew the complaints all too well, as I myself was making them only six months earlier. I waved my arms wildly to try and calm the rebellion, protesting that this was not what I was proposing. We were making so much noise by this point that quite a few people in the pub were looking over at our table, wondering what on earth was going on. Eventually I was able to move on to my presentation proper, and proceeded to reveal my new brand positioning of which I was so proud. Box by box I revealed the work, going through the benefits, brand truths, brand personality and then the 'brand idea', as a summary of the whole thing. I sat back and waited for the applause to break out, but was met with stony silence. After what felt like an eternity, Pete mumbled something I didn't pick up, as he was looking down into his beer. He finally looked up, fixed me with a cold stare and repeated himself, his words hitting me like arrows from a bow. He said I'd become 'one of them'. I didn't need any more explanation to know what he meant. In his eyes I'd become a fancy-pants marketing man, with clever charts and big words, miles away from the reality of life in the supermarket trenches.

Tessa went to get a round of drinks in whilst I closed my laptop down. She came back with four pints of beer and one bright pink cocktail with a little umbrella. I knew she wouldn't be seen dead drinking anything pink; there was only one person the cocktail was for. I could tell by the glint in her eye that she was mentally pulling ahead of me in the race for the Sales Director job, leaving me in her wake and kicking dust in my face. All my enthusiasm had waned, and I felt well and truly depressed. I was cocking up my new job in brand management at the same time as giving my competitor for the Sales Director's seat a leg up.

TESCO DIRECT (WEDNESDAY, JUNE 6)

Got an unexpected call today, just as I got home from work. It was William Dawson, a headhunter who used to contact me on a regular basis, but eventually gave up when he saw I was planning to stay at Simpton's. He was as slimy as an oil slick, but very well connected in the Sales and Marketing world. He thought I might be ripe for picking and re-planting in pastures new.

The explanation for the sudden re-kindling of interest in me was rather worrying; it was no coincidence that his call came only days after my disastrous brand positioning pub test. Word of my less than smooth move to brand management had reached him, as had rumours that the Sales Director's seat was being kept warm for Tessa Williams. I felt like Amy at her last birthday party, when she lost concentration during the final phase of musical chairs and was beaten to the last cushion by a pushy plump girl from her school. I contemplated copying her reaction – locking myself in the bedroom and refusing to come out. Instead, I feigned interest, expecting him to pitch me on becoming assistant to the deputy buyer at Kwiksave based in Rochdale, or some other equally enticing 'opportunity'.

But when I heard what he had on offer, I sat down heavily on the stairs with a thump. I let forth a string of expletives, causing Amy to stare at me with accusing eyes before running into the kitchen to report me to the swearing police. This was not any old job. This was a shot at becoming the head of food buying for none other than Tesco, reporting directly to the Commercial Director. They wanted to meet me next week for a first interview, and were keen to move fast. It seemed they took the fact of me being given a brand management job as proof of strategic skills and broader business understanding. This was stretching things a little, but then as I like to say, 'Never let the truth get in the way of a good story'.

I discussed the Tesco opportunity with Claire over dinner, and when I told her about the generous salary package she quickly forgave me for trebling Amy's vocabulary of naughty words in one fell swoop. She gobbled down her food, grabbed her glass of wine, asked me to clear up and then went off to gaze longingly at the brochures for kitchen extensions she had been collecting. I might as well arrange for the new salary to be Direct Debited straight to the local builders. I surprised myself by being less sure about the Tesco job, despite its many attractions. My time in brand management had been far from easy and my first stumbling steps were like Bambi the deer trying to ice skate. But now I felt that I was getting somewhere, learning something and, dare I say it, even starting to enjoy the whole branding thing. It felt too soon to give it up and jump ship.

SELL THE CAKE, NOT THE RECIPE (FRIDAY, JUNE 8)

Tonight we went out to Jamie Oliver's restaurant 15 for Claire's birthday and I got my own present, in the form of an idea about how I should be bringing to life the brand vision. The restaurant is the one featured in the TV programme called Jamie's Kitchen where he tried to transform 15 disaffected, unemployed 'yoofs' into chefs. I'd been sceptical about how good the food could be when the people making it were unable to string together one sensible sentence, and didn't recognize a cucumber. But I guess he'd trained them well, or quietly fired them all after filming had finished and hired some real chefs, as the nosh was top-notch.

One of Claire's friends works for the production company who made his TV programmes, and I'd asked her if she could fix it for Jamie to come to our table for a chat. She'd also ensured we booked on one of the rare nights when he was actually in the kitchen. We were waiting for our desserts and there was no sign of the cheeky chappie; I was starting to give up hope. But then I saw him burst out of the kitchen with a chocolate cake topped off with a sparkler. Claire almost wet herself when he asked her to budge up and make room for him. He chatted to us for a full 10 minutes, bubbling with effervescent enthusiasm about the 15 restaurants he was opening in Cornwall and New York. He also waxed lyrical about the chocolate cake we were eating. He nicked a bit of mine and closed his eyes as he wafted off on a flying carpet of chocolate pleasure. He described how he loved the contrast of dark chocolate topping, milk chocolate sponge and white chocolate sauce. And this is when the brand idea popped into my head. Jamie hadn't come out and explained how he had made the cake, or at what temperature he had cooked it. No, he presented the cake with a bit of theatre, and then concentrated on why it tasted so great.

In contrast, I had become obsessed with the 'recipe' for my brand, agonising over every last word in the strategy, rather than focusing on the 'cake' of what the brand would look and feel like. The piss-taking in the pub was spot on: I'd caught Hugo-itis and become far too intellectual in my approach. I needed to think less, and do more, working on bringing to life the vision and what it meant for the business. How would we change the packaging and product? What new products would we create? It was a similar story to the one I saw in the focus groups when consumers looked blankly at the concept boards for our pizza launch.

GET STUCK IN (MONDAY, JUNE 11)

Inspired by Jamie Oliver and his orgasmic chocolate cake, I wanted to get stuck in and work on bringing the Simpton's brand to life. I could see this helping us in several ways. First, we'd bring to life the strategy in a way that would pass the pub test. Second, we would be able to explore the brand idea with consumers much more effectively than with the sort of dry concept boards used on the pizza project. Finally, and most importantly, we'd have a few ideas for real-life projects we might actually launch, assuming I could somehow raid the pizza launch fund for some money. Rather than just thinking about the brand and waiting till later to actually do anything, we were doing both at the same time.

Hugo was off on a European tour meeting the final designers in the Pizzart design competition, so this afternoon I organized a half-day workshop, not just a lunchtime meeting. I hadn't expected Jane to join us, as she was supposed to be with Hugo. However, she'd managed to wriggle her way out of the trip, which was good to see.

I started by sharing the story of my pub-test experience, and how the strategy had gone down as well as a male stripper at a nuns' convention. Brian slid even further down in his chair than normal on hearing the bad news, so only his head was visible above the table. But I quickly went on to explain what we needed to do. I held up with one hand the recipe for chocolate cake I'd found in Jamie Oliver's book. I then revealed a real choco-late cake I'd made earlier, and asked the team which was more appealing. The team hesitated but eventually plumped for the cake. My baking skills leave something to be desired, and Claire had refused to join in my midnight cake-making frenzy when we got back from 15, but I just about got my point across.

We used a series of five exercises to generate ideas, getting the team to note down their thoughts on Post-it notes:

1. What's wrong with our products today, and how could we make them better?

2. What things are going on in the life of our consumer, Sarah, beyond just sausages or even food?
3. Looking at other markets and brands outside our category, what good ideas can we steal?
4. Pick your favourite bit of the new brand positioning, and use this as stimulus for ideas.
5. Think about your own experience using the product, and how we could make this better.

Within an hour I was amazed to see that each of us had a daisy-chain of Post-its with product ideas; it seemed this brand vision thing really was good at helping us to come up with ideas. We stuck the ideas up and grouped them into product families, then sat back down and wondered what to do next. Jane suggested asking, for each idea, how well they brought to life our vision and how big we thought they'd be in sales terms. At first I waited for the other ten criteria I thought she was going to propose as part of some complex evaluation system, but she didn't. That was it. Does it build the brand and does it build the business? It seemed my search for simplicity was rubbing off on Jane as well, and I winked at her to show my approval.

Jane went up to the flipchart and drew the four boxes to evaluate the product ideas and we moved the Post-its onto this page (Figure 6.1). It was clear that there were three big ideas that stood out. First was the idea of re-launching our current sausages with the 'original recipe'. This sounded easy, but was a big job as we'd need to undo all of Hugo's handiwork of the last couple of years. Second was a range of special sausages from different regions of the country, called 'Farmers' Select'. For each of these we'd create a partnership with a particular producer, and tell their story on the pack. By showing the actual farmer who had made your sausages, you'd be confident you were getting a high-quality product with the bonus of feeling it had a personal touch. The final product idea was a bit off-the-wall, but could actually work. It came from Brian, who had decided to 'swing both ways' in dietary terms, eating lots of veggie food but also the occasional bit of meat. He'd even gone out and bought a barbeque from B&Q and invited some mates over. When it pissed down with rain he was determined to go ahead, and so started a new trend of indoor barbequing. This resulted in the local fire brigade paying a visit, but did trigger the creation of Brian's big idea. He found his sausages had the annoying habit of rolling around on the grill, making it hard to cook them evenly. Even worse was the tendency of the sausages to roll all the way off and fall into the charcoal or on the floor. So, he came up with the idea for… square sausages. It seemed strange at first, and I was sure Ron would have a cardiac arrest

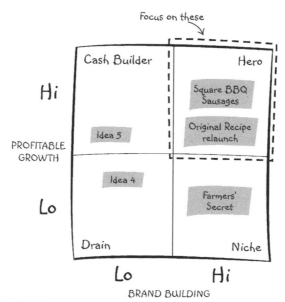

Figure 6.1: Picking the product ideas with promise

at the thought of modifying the production line to make square sausages. But what the hell.

Finally, we came up with a powerful promotional idea that tapped into our mission to get families eating together again. The idea was to campaign for a 'Simpton's Sunday' where families would enjoy an English breakfast, with Simpton's sausages in a starring role.

The meeting broke up and I sat down with Jane to get her advice on what to do next. Clearly we had to do more to bring the ideas to life and not rely on written statements. She'd wanted to do what she called 'mock-ups' of packaging, but when she talked to INK about doing this they gave her a quote for £20 000 and said it would take four to five weeks to complete. There was no way Hugo was going to give me two grand, never mind twenty. And what's more, if I went to him with our plans he'd not only refuse to feed the little birds in our nest of our ideas; he'd stamp on them with his storm-trooper's boots. Well, at least I could talk to Ron at the factory to work on some product prototypes. And we'd try and figure out a way to get some pack designs worked up.

TESCO TEMPTATION (THURSDAY, JUNE 14)

Spent a whole day on 'holiday' having a series of tough but interesting interviews with Tesco. And I must admit that if they decide to offer me a job, it would be hard to turn them down. It would be a big step up financially, but beyond the kitchen extension-enabling angle, it would be a great move career-wise. The Commercial Director was what I would expect from Tesco: direct to the point of being blunt, but focused on moving the business forward. I also liked their obsession with focusing only on things that helped them achieve their mission of 'winning the life-long loyalty of their customer'. If it didn't help them do this, they cut it out. They were also very ambitious, with plans to grow the UK business, but also expanding abroad and of course, online. They said they were seeing 5 other candidates, and that I should find out their decision in the next 2-3 weeks.

DESIGN FOR DADS (TUESDAY, JUNE 19)

This morning I might have found a way to get our new ideas mocked up, through one of the Dads at Amy's school. He and I are about the only parents who walk with our kids, rather than dropping them off in the line of 4x4's that fill the curved driveway in front of the school. I'm waiting for the day when one of the Mums kicks her kids out of the Range Rover while it's still moving, getting them to jump and roll like Starsky and Hutch, so she can get to her tennis lesson five minutes earlier. (I have a well-balanced attitude to private education and posh people. I have a chip on each shoulder.) Anyway, this other Dad works in a small design agency and when I mentioned my prototype predicament he offered to get one of his trainees to have a bash, in return for a supply of sausages for the firm's summer party. I accepted his offer on the spot, and promised to email a brief later today.

TASTING IS BELIEVING (THURSDAY, JUNE 21)

Headed up to the factory today, and this time Brian and Jane joined me in a team road-trip. Jane confided to me that she is finding it hard to stay motivated on the pizza project, but is scared to face up to Hugo. My first impression of her was that she was confident to the point of being cocky. But in fact, beneath the surface she's actually quite insecure.

Ron and his team had done us proud. We arrived at the factory just in time for lunch, and were shown straight through to the canteen. It turns out that rather than making one or two samples as I had expected, they had made enough for the whole factory to have a taste! It was a real thrill to see the recipes we had worked on only weeks earlier actually coming to life before our eyes and taste buds. A long trestle table had been set up, and there were plates of hot, steaming sausages ready to taste. I helped myself to a couple of Original Recipe ones, which were even better than the ones Ron had sent me a month ago. He explained that he'd fine-tuned the ingredient list on the advice of a secret advisor.

Brian saw there was a barbeque outside and set off to see if his square sausages had also seen the light of day. He came back smiling from ear to ear, holding two door-step slices of bread sandwiching what did indeed look like two square sausages. He told me the barbeque was doing a roaring trade and that he had really hit on a genuine source of frustration amongst barbequers. Like Jane, Brian also seemed to be getting a bit more into the product, and was actually enjoying being separated from his PC for more than an hour at a time. Ron did confirm that it would be a nightmare to fix up the factory to make the product, but he was up for having a go having seen the rapturous reaction of the canteen guinea pigs.

I looked outside at the people manning the barbeque and could have sworn that one of them looked familiar. When I walked outside I was amazed to see it was none other than Old Mr Simpton himself. He looked like a jolly Father Christmas who had landed six months early, with his white beard and rotund figure. He was clearly having a ball. I went over to say hello, half expecting him not to remember me, but he put down his spatula and shook my hand vigorously. He thanked me for my work, saying that he hadn't seen the place as animated as this for years, and definitely not since his nephew had taken the reins of the company. Seeing the queue for square sausages had dwindled, he took off his apron and asked me to follow him. He bounded up three flights of stairs, leaving me gasping in his wake. I jogged to catch up with him when he reached the third and top floor of the building. I walked into his office, which was big but modest for a Company Chairman. He lifted a painting of the new factory being opened back in the 1900s to reveal a safe. He opened it and then ceremoniously retrieved a well-worn, leather-bound book that he handed to me. I opened it carefully and found inside a sheaf of papers yellowed with age, and frayed from being consulted many times. The handwriting was hard to decipher, but I could see that it recorded what looked like a series of different recipes. On about the tenth page was an entry circled in red ink. I looked up to see Old Mr Simpton beaming brightly and then it clicked. I was looking at the original Simpton's recipe from over a hundred years ago. So now I knew who Ron's secret recipe advisor was! He took the book and locked it safely back in its hiding place. He patted me on the shoulder as I left his office, and offered his help in getting my ideas off the ground. For the first time I felt like the brand vision and product ideas were more than just an exercise in the impossible. We might actually be able to pull them off for real.

Ron agreed to work on a plan of what it would take to make the new products we'd come up with, in addition to a more detailed cost estimate. Brian, Jane and I headed off with our bellies full of food and our heads bursting with ideas for our re-launch.

NEW DESIGNS ON OUR FUTURE (WEDNESDAY, JUNE 27)

The month ended on a real high with the design ideas from Phil, the Dad at Amy's school. Phil had started by looking at the packaging designs that were in the advertising history I'd given to him as part of my 'brief' brief. He'd taken some stills from the adverts and been able to do a little history of the pack design over the years, and it told the same sorry story as with the brand's communication. For years the brand had stuck to having the same stuff on the pack, or 'visual identity' as Phil called it. For 20 years or so the star of the design was the founder of the company, George Simpton himself. He looked like the archetypal old English country gent, with big handle-bar moustache and bushy eyebrows. There was also the family crest, and the proud statement of 'Original recipe since 1830'. As with the advertising, with the arrival of Jonathan Simpton the design had changed radically. Out had gone George Simpton and the family crest, jettisoned by the new kid on the block, in favour of a more modern and minimalist design with tastefully shot sausage photos. Phil told me that a famous fashion photo-grapher had been hired at great expense to take the pictures. We'd even been a sponsor of London Fashion Week to launch the new pack designs; so that's where Hugo got the inspiration for his Tate Modern design idea. Shame that the supermarket shoppers I saw shunning our brand weren't aware of this, and couldn't care less anyway. What struck me is that by ditching our brand heritage and putting fancy photos on the pack we now looked like a clone of the own label brands, who also had nice pictures of the product.

Phil and his team proposed to re-introduce the brand 'prop-erties' we'd lost, but give them a modern twist. They proposed using a caricature-style illustration of George Simpton, like one of the old cartoons you sometimes see that exaggerate a person's features. The company crest had also been dusted down and put back in pride of place. What really sold me on the design was a clever trick that Phil used to show two views of the supermarket sausage shelf. The first was how things look today, with us drowning invisibly in a sea of sausage photos. But in the second, with the new design, we stuck out much more and shouted for attention. At least this way we had a chance of people picking us up for a second look, and that was half the battle. I think his agency deserved a lifetime supply of Simpton's sausages, not just enough for their summer barbeque.

I feel I'm ready to go back into the lions' den of the pub positioning test. If I can't pull it off with the prototype mix I've developed then it's time to call it quits. I'm now impatient to hear from Tesco about their job offer, as I might really need it.

JUNE'S SUMMARY

1. Avoid becoming focused on the strategy itself and becoming too intellectual about branding: try to 'think less, and do more'.

2. Using the brand vision as a 'trampoline' for idea creation delivers a double whammy: you bring to life your ideas and get some good ideas for innovation.

3. Think like an entrepreneur when mocking up ideas. Hunt around and you'll find ways of doing this work well on the cheap.

Quarter Three

TEST-DRIVING THE VISION

7.

July – Show them the money (selling the vision to management)

CRUNCHING THE NUMBERS (TUESDAY, JULY 3)

We've made good progress with creating a vision for the brand and started to bring it to life with concrete ideas. But to go further we now need to sell our vision to the company's management. And the time to do this is approaching fast in the shape of the annual budget review, run by Hugo and Jonathan Simpton, the CEO.

From my experience in sales I knew that the key on presenting to top management was making a strong business case. We needed to avoid too much clever stuff on the brand, and focus on showing how our ideas would help us boost profits, as if we were pitching a business idea to potential investors.

Jane offered to start putting together a more detailed plan and budget for the re-launch. We set some rough objectives around winning back some of the consumers we'd lost to the retailer brands, or 're-trial' to use the jargon. Our aim was to get 10% of the UK's sausage buyers to try us again. With our new improved product, we were aiming for a bigger bunch of these to buy again, compared with the current situation. We knew that we wouldn't be able to afford TV advertising, as this would be way too expensive. So Jane said she would look at a plan that used a mix of advertising in women's magazines and online on food and cooking websites. The other important part of the financial plan was product costs, which Ron had sent through. The good news was that he could make the original recipe sausages for only 10% more, thanks to some clever cost-saving ideas his team had come up with. It seems that the people at the factory were really behind our plans to re-launch the sausage business, seeing it as a way to help fight for their own future and save their jobs.

Still no news from Tesco, and the headhunter William Dawson is not returning my calls. Suggests I have not got the job, and so I really need to do a good job at selling my plans in the pub test later this week.

PUB TEST – THE RE-MATCH (MONDAY, JULY 9)

Back from the pub and I feel like I've scored the winning goal in the FA Cup Final (or at least the Putney Sunday League Dads five-a-side knockout). I reconvened the same group who had peed all over my brand bonfire last time, and took them through the re-launch manifesto, product, packaging and promotion. The reaction could not have been more different than my first attempt. They loved the new packaging, sharing my belief that it would stop sausage shoppers in their tracks. They thought that going back to the original recipe was smart, as retailers were looking to raise quality and deliver more natural, authentic products. And they liked the Simpton's Sunday campaign. They even found the manifesto quite good, as it was written in language they could understand, not brand-speak. What's more, when they had seen the ideas, they were all able to play back the brand vision more or less. And not a single Power-Point slide was in sight. The only slight worry of the evening was Tessa's comment that I might actually have a career in brand management, and that a return to sales was perhaps no longer on the horizon. I had a vivid image of her squeezing herself into the Sales Director's chair and putting her feet up on the desk.

With the positive reaction from tonight I think I'm ready to climb the next mountain, this time an Everest-like challenge. I need to try and sell Hugo on the re-launch and force open his tightly clenched fist that holds all the money.

SOHO HOUSE SALE (MONDAY, JULY 16)

I was expecting Hugo to throw a fit when he heard my plans, so when choosing the place for our meeting I took a tip out of my favourite movie, Jerry McGuire. In the film Jerry gets fired in a crowded restaurant so he's too embarrassed to make a scene. There was only one choice for my meeting: Soho House. But in the end the lunch went well, perhaps too well to be true.

I showed Hugo the same re-launch plans as in my pub test, using the product, packaging and promotion, and waited for him to choke on his Caesar Salad (no anchovies, with the sauce on the side). But instead he just nodded his head, held up his glass of Chardonnay and proposed a toast to me. I nervously clinked my glass of over-priced mineral water, half expecting him to come to his senses and spit out his wine. He didn't even flinch when I said I was looking for £2 million of marketing funds for the sausage re-launch. This paled in comparison with the pizza launch plan, but was still a big bag of money. But even this failed to faze him. He told me that my work behind the scenes of the core business was Simpsational. It meant that we would have 'a balanced portfolio of product launches with different risk profiles and different long-term cash-flow generating potential'. I think this means one safe but boring bet (my sausages) and one sexy, exciting gamble that could be much bigger if it came off (his pizza).

I didn't hang around for dessert, deciding it was best to escape before Hugo had a chance to change his mind. As I was leaving, I saw a tall, red-haired woman entering the ladies' room: Tessa. I hid behind a plant pot and waited for her to emerge. Unfortunately, when she did come out she was staring straight at me, and clearly my hiding place left something to be desired. She waved hello and strode over, asking if potted plants were another interest I'd picked up during my time in brand management. I said 'get lost hippo-hips', at least in my head. The words that actually came out of my mouth said how nice it was to see her, and enquired about who she was meeting. She replied cryptically that she was seeing a new friend, spun on her stilettos and strode off. I risked being detected again by stalking her at a distance, following her back to the dining room. I got there just in time to see her air-kissing none other than Hugo Gaines. What was that all about, I wondered? And did it have anything to do with why Hugo bought my plan without a struggle?

As I left Soho House I got a call from the headhunters about the Tesco job. And would you believe it, I got it. What a result. William Dawson said they wanted a quick decision, at the latest in a week's time, but I'm really in two minds about what I should do. On the one hand, Tessa gives the impression she's got the Sales Director's job at Simpton's sewn up, which isn't good for my prospects. And there is the matter of Claire's kitchen extension; she's already picked out the new, bigger table and chairs to fill it. But I finally feel like I'm getting somewhere in brand management and, though I hate to admit it, I'm actually enjoying it. Packing it in now when I'm on the verge of getting my plan approved just doesn't feel right.

THE BUDGET MEETING BECKONS (MONDAY, JULY 23)

It's *show* time. Tomorrow is the budget meeting, when I have to pitch the sausage re-launch plan to Jonathan Simpton, the CEO. Extra support came from an unexpected source, in the shape of Ron from the factory. He'd come all the way down from Manchester to wish me good luck in person. He'd also delivered by hand some fresh samples of the new products, wanting to see them arrive safely with his own eyes. He would work in the kitchen tomorrow to get them cooked just at the right time so they were piping hot.

I am nervous about the meeting, but confident in our plans. And I feel I have to see them through now we've come so far. So I spent an hour writing and re-writing an email to William Dawson at the headhunters trying to politely turn down the Tesco job. Twice I hit 'Send', only to feel a rising sense of panic, scrabbling to hit the Cancel button. Finally, on my third attempt, I plucked up the courage to go through with it, and, with a feeling of trepidation, I heard the 'ping' of the email setting off on its journey.

I went out for a team dinner with Jane and Brian, to say thanks for all their support. It's great to see that they are right behind me, a real transformation compared with when I arrived back in January. Jane still has to work on the pizza launch, but after a few too many glasses of wine she admitted that its chances of success are limited to say the least. She feels like a movie director who has just watched the first screening of her new film and knows deep down that it's a turkey. But the screens are booked and the show has to go on. What she does believe in is our sausage re-launch plan. We shared a taxi home, and I was flattered but a bit un-nerved when she asked me in for a coffee. I was on the point of accepting when my better judgement shouted through the alcoholic haze to go straight home, pronto.

AMBUSH! (TUESDAY, JULY 24)

Just out of the budget meeting during a break caused by Jonathan Simpton having to take an important call. I have a terrible urge to run out of the building and not stop till I get home. How could I have been so blind not to see the ambush that I walked straight into this morning?

Before the meeting had even started my hands were sweating and my heart was beating like a heavy metal drummer doing a solo. I was seated at one end of a long mahogany table, with Jane by my side. At the other end of the table was the firing squad of Jonathan Simpton, my old mate Marcus from HR, Hugo and Tessa Williams who was sitting in for the Sales Director. Hugo and Tessa both looked as smug as a pair of cats who'd treated themselves to a tetra-pack of cream each. Looking back now, I should have known something was up.

Jane sailed through the pizza launch plan like a boat at the Henley Regatta, waved on enthusiastically by Jonathan Simpton. She even got a round of applause at the end of her presentation. However, it was a different story altogether when it was my time to talk. I went through my well-rehearsed pitch that showed the business rationale for re-investing on the core business. Jonathan Simpton took out a huge cigar and lit it, in blatant disregard of the company's no-smoking policy. He leaned back his head and blew a large plume of smoke up towards the ceiling; my sausage re-launch plan suffered the same fate moments later. He growled that I was trying to take us back into yesteryear when I should be joining Hugo in his brave march towards a Simpsational future. Hugo beamed proudly and nodded his agreement, without even a word of support for me. I cursed under my breath as he then proceeded to deliver the killer blow by explaining that I'd worked on the plan behind his back, something I couldn't argue with, as it was at least partly true. All I could say is that the project was a solo effort and didn't involve Jane or Brian. Jane was about to protest, but I kicked her under the table just in time.

I tried in vain to get Brian's help as a computer superman to retrieve the email I'd sent to William Dawson, but to no avail. And I don't have the heart to call and grovel for him to re-consider my rejection of the Tesco job.

SURVIVING THE SHIPWRECK (WEDNESDAY, JULY 25)

Woke up on the sofa this morning with one hell of a hangover after one (or more like ten) too many celebratory drinks with Jane last night. I feel like the heavy metal drum soloist has moved into my head, and our cat with the sensitive tummy has spent the night sleeping on my tongue. Claire was far from sympathetic, complaining that I was spending more nights with Jane than with her at the moment. Well, at least our sausage plan is still alive, albeit in a scaled-down form.

I was called back in to the budget meeting yesterday and Jonathan Simpton was about to officially pronounce my plans dead and buried, when the boardroom doors burst open dramatically and in marched Old Mr Simpton. He grabbed the cigar from his nephew's mouth and stuck it in his glass of Evian, before pulling him up by the collar like a naughty schoolboy who'd been caught stealing apples. He then sat down in Jonathan's forcibly vacated chair. As the doors swung shut I caught a quick glimpse of Ron smiling from ear to ear and giving me the thumbs up.

Old Mr Simpton barked at Jonathan to summarize the discussion so far. The CEO sheepishly explained that he had just cancelled the sausage re-launch plan. At this point there was a knock at the door and Ron walked in, head held high, proudly holding a silver platter full of steaming sausages. Old Mr Simpton asked if Jonathan had actually tasted Ron's handiwork, and then proceeded to ask the same question of the rest of the firing squad. Each of them reddened in turn like the sequence of traffic lights you see at the start of a Formula One race, as they meekly shook their heads. With a flourish, the Chairman stuck a fork into one of the sausages and took a big bite, munching away contentedly. He finished eating, wiped his white beard with a cloth and said that this was the best sausage he had tasted since he was a boy.

Hugo protested that there wasn't an extra £2 million to spare for my re-launch plans, and was backed up by the Finance Director. Old Mr Simpton reluctantly agreed that budgets were tight. Even though he had his doubts about the pizza launch, they had promised customers and shareholders that it would be launched with a bang, and had even revealed how much would be spent on it.

It was Jane who came up with the plan that kept us in the game. She suggested doing a test market of our sausage re-launch plans in one part of the country. We had a regional supermarket with whom we could partner, and regional news-papers could be used for the promotion in the place of wom-en's magazines. In this way we could test out our plans on a small scale, with 20% of the original budget. Old Mr Simpton congratulated Jane on her idea, and looked each of the board members in the eye, one by one, asking them if they agreed. They all nodded, causing the Chairman to smile for the first time that morning.

In addition to being pleased about saving our sausage plan, I'm also happy that I told Hugo what I thought about him outside the meeting room. I'd held back all year from saying what I really thought; after all, he was my boss. But this time he'd gone too far. I told him he was a two-timing, double-crossing dick-head. I was shocked to see that Old Mr Simpton had overheard my comments, and was about to apologize to Hugo. But before I could, the old man chimed in 'Well said, my boy'.

JULY'S SUMMARY

1. Don't under-estimate the challenge of selling your plans in-ternally. Getting people in the business on your side is es-sential.
2. In particular, without support from top management your brand vision will be a waste of time.
3. When selling to senior management, make sure you 'show them the money': make the business case for your ideas, and cut back on the clever marketing theory.

8.

August – Consumer test drive (exploring the brand ideas with consumers)

BRAND IDOL (THURSDAY, AUGUST 2)

Having got some good feedback from people inside the business on our ideas, it was now time to see if consumers shared our enthusiasm: we needed to take our vision for a test drive. Hugo wouldn't be joining us, as he is on a drive of his own, down to the French Riviera in his Porsche Boxster. Shelly asked with a sly grin if it was a coincidence that Marcus from HR was also going there for his holiday. Hugo looked surprisingly smug before leaving, given that his plans to sabotage the sausage plan had failed. This suggests he's got more tricks up his sleeve, and I think I need to watch my back even more carefully from now on.

I want to avoid the mistakes I'd seen in how consumer research was done on the pizza project. First, we mustn't rely on research for the answers. We should have a point of view about what will work, based on our insight into the consumer, brand and competition. Research can then help deepen our insight and understanding. I want the team to develop the same 'nose for a hit' in marketing that Simon Cowell has when judging singers on the X-Factor and American Idol. From experience built up over many years he has an intuitive sense about what the public will buy. The second thing I want to avoid is researching complicated, wordy ideas presented in the artificial 'hot-house' environment of a focus group. Instead, I want to carry on with the approach of using prototype products and marketing ideas to explore our ideas.

Jane came across an interesting company at a conference who are called, rather aptly, Everyday Lives. Rather than doing focus groups, they spend time with people in their homes or out and about, filming them as they go about their lives. **They'd used this for the coffee brand Kenco who were looking at the out-of-home coffee market** (wheresthesausage.com). They found that cappuccino drinkers were as concerned about the cup, spoon and froth as they were about the coffee itself. Kenco sold only the coffee beans, but needed to help the café owners they worked with to improve the presentation of the drink as well. The Kenco team also got a video presentation of the insights at the end of the project. This was a damn sight more interesting than the normal dry and dull research debrief, and more effective at communicating the insights inside the company. We plan to start with three filmed in-home weekend visits exploring our re-launch stuff, learn from this, and then go back and do three more sessions the following weekend.

THE INK POT IS EMPTY (TUESDAY, AUGUST 7)

Jane showed me the five best designs in the Pizzart competition, selected from all the pizza box design ideas we had received. There was a graffiti-style design, one with an oriental theme and the three others I struggle to describe. I was tempted to say that I thought Amy's school art project was more professional, but could see that Jane felt bad enough as it was already. When I asked her how many entries there had been altogether she blushed. The total number of entries was actually only three, with INK having to knock up a couple of designs of their own to get up to five. But this was still only half the number of designs needed for the Pizzart event at Tate Modern. As a result Hugo had no choice but to cancel the show, as the gallery would have been almost empty.

Jane also showed me the storyboard for the pizza launch TV advertising. ETC had stuck with their original idea of the 'pizza of the stars', only it seems that Kate Moss wasn't that keen on starring in a Simpton's pizza advert. So instead we would have some Z-list celebrity called Brandy. No second name, just Brandy. Shelly reliably informed me that her claim to fame was coming third on 'I'm a Celebrity, Get Me Out of Here'. This is probably what she'll be screaming when filming of the advert starts, as it is so cringe-worthy. The words in the advert go something like:

'You eat in the best restaurants.
You go to the hottest clubs.
You drink the finest wine.
So don't settle for second best when it comes to pizza.
Be Simpsational.'

The only person in the team who seems excited about the advert is Shelly, as she is hoping to go along to the shoot and snap Brandy and any other celebs who show up on her snazzy new pink mobile phone camera.

Seeing the pizza packs and advertising reminded me that I needed to talk to the agencies and brief them to produce materials for family weekend research next week. I first called INK, but they said they were tied up on the pizza launch till after the summer. It was the same answer with ETC. It's my hunch that Hugo was actually responsible for this sudden lack of resource, briefing the agencies to not help us out. I was saved by the agency run by Phil, the Dad from Amy's school. He put us in touch with a small start-up advertising agency called Zebra that had an office in the same building, and who can help us out.

EVERYDAY LIVES (MONDAY, AUGUST 13)

We spent most of yesterday on one of the home visits, with Jane, Brian and I attending a session each. We got together this morning for a chat about what we had found out, and all agreed it was by a long stretch the most interesting and useful market research we had seen. It was refreshing to see real people living their real lives, or as real as it can be when you are being filmed on a video camera and you have a nosey marketing person asking you questions. But after a while we learnt not to ask for an explanation for the slightest of actions, and the consumers started to forget about the fact they were being filmed.

Overall, the stuff we showed to people worked well and was well received. The two agencies had done a great job in bringing our ideas to life. They'd done a series of mocked-up press adverts that announced the return to the original Simpton's recipe and introduced the new products, using the slogan of 'Come home to the real taste of Simpton's'.

The families we talked to were fed up with so many food brands being pretentious and fancy. You could no longer sell pork, it had to be hand-reared, free-range, lovingly cared for, special breed pork. So, the idea of a brand that was going back to basics, and reviving traditional values, was appreciated. They also agreed that the occasional fry-up or barbeque was enjoyable, fun and perfectly OK as long as you treated it as a treat, and not your daily diet. They were tired of being preached at by scaremongering government ministers and brands. The new product ideas went down well, with the square sausages in particular a big hit.

But the biggest and most exciting thing we found out was about our target audience. We had started with Mums in mind, and this was reflected in our choice of magazines for the mock-up of the Simpton's Sunday campaign: *Elle*, *Hello*! and the like. However, in all three families we noticed how when it came to the cooked breakfast or the barbeque, it was the Dads who took charge. When we discussed this with the families, we found out that these sorts of meals were just about the only ones where most Dads took the lead. They were especially important moments, as the traditional Sunday roast was now in terminal decline. Spending time with the families also reinforced the insight about how rare it is for families to eat together. We'd read the data that Brian had found on the internet about this issue, but seeing people rush around, grabbing solo snacks made this much more vivid. All the families agreed that when they did eat together, they really enjoyed it, especially when the meal was something like sausage, bacon and egg that everyone loved, including the kids.

TIME FOR ACTION (WEDNESDAY, AUGUST 15)

We spent the last two days having a meeting in a country hotel not far from the office, to finalize our brand ideas and action plans. What a difference compared with the Babbington House brand blow-up I went to earlier in the year. This workshop was much more about action, and less about buzzwords and brand bollocks. In addition to Jane, Brian and me we had invited Ron down from the factory, John from Sales and one person each from the design and communication agencies. That way they would help us finalize the brand idea, and so hopefully have a better understanding of it.

We kicked off the session with the presentation from the Everyday Lives team. They had produced a 30-minute movie that dramatized the key findings from the family visits, and whilst it was no Tom Cruise blockbuster, it had us all enthralled. Seeing for yourself how a typical family ate mostly by themselves, in a fragmented fashion, really rammed home the insight about the breakdown in family mealtimes. Hearing how good old Simpton's bangers could indeed help reform the family circle confirmed that our insight had tapped into something important. It was also inspiring to see the reactions of people trying out the new products like the square and original recipe sausages reacting enthusiastically. We captured our key findings on Post-its, and then stuck them up, as we had now got used to doing. I was able to summarize the main changes to make to the positioning, with the biggest one being the fine-tuning of the target.

I made the changes to the positioning over lunch, adding a longer-hand version of the brand idea to make it clearer, and creating an extra box for the key plans to emphasize the need for action (Figure 8.1) and then in the afternoon we went through the brand idea and evaluated it. I asked people to answer four key questions:

- Is it MOTIVATING for you as a team?
- Will it be MOTIVATING for our consumers?
- Is it DIFFERENT from what the competition are doing?
- It is TRUE and credible?

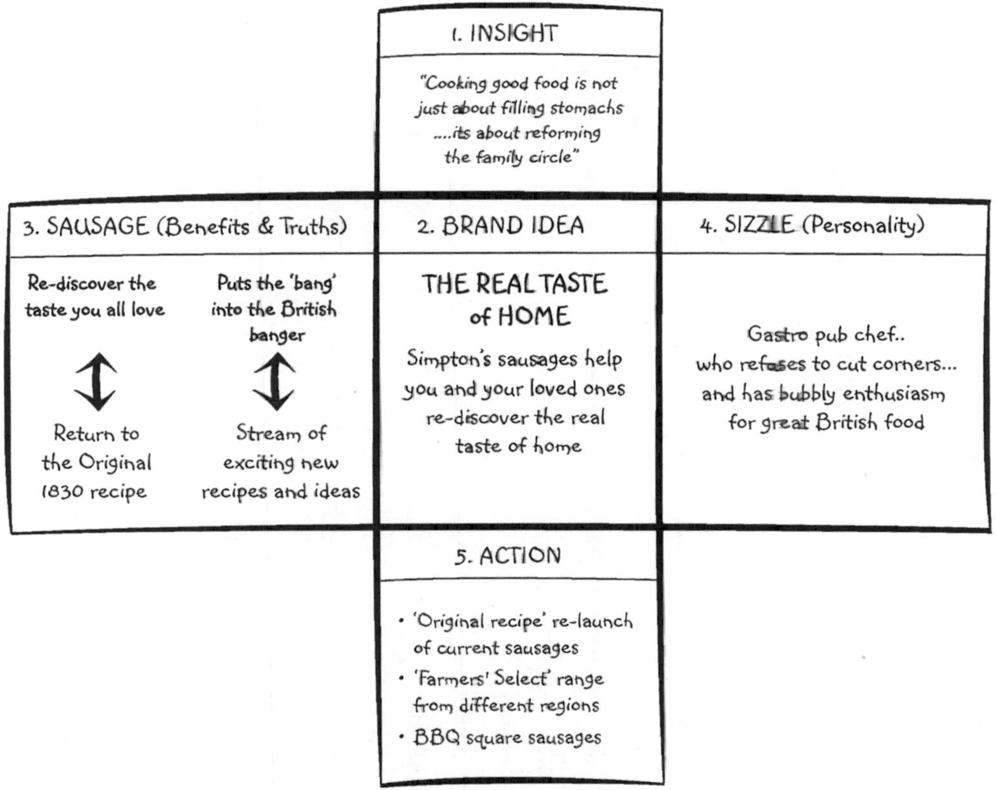

1. INSIGHT

"Cooking good food is not just about filling stomachs ...its about reforming the family circle"

2. BRAND IDEA

THE REAL TASTE of HOME

Simpton's sausages help you and your loved ones re-discover the real taste of home

3. SAUSAGE (Benefits & Truths)

Re-discover the taste you all love ⟷ Puts the 'bang' into the British banger

Return to the Original 1830 recipe ⟷ Stream of exciting new recipes and ideas

4. SIZZLE (Personality)

Gastro pub chef.. who refuses to cut corners... and has bubbly enthusiasm for great British food

5. ACTION

- 'Original recipe' re-launch of current sausages
- 'Farmers' Select' range from different regions
- BBQ square sausages

Figure 8.1: Final Brand Idea for Simpton's

We felt that we did pretty well on the first two questions, which we scored at 8 out of 10. It was less strong on credibility, with 7 out of 10, as we felt we really needed Ron and his team to deliver the products to support it. And the weakest score of all was for differentiation, where we gave ourselves a 6, feeling that the retail own label brands were quite close to where we wanted to be. However, John pointed out that a large part of differentiation was going to come from how well we executed the vision. And when I thought about my favourite brands, like innocent and Apple, I could see he was right. Smart strategy was part of the battle, but so was having fantastic packaging, design and communication that helped us stand out. We would need to do a lot more work on that. We agreed that the positioning was 90% there and that there was no point wasting any more time on fiddling with the words. We were better off using it and finding out if it worked.

On the second day we moved into action planning mode. I stuck a series of flipcharts on the wall to create a huge calendar, with the next two years broken down quarter by quarter (Figure 8.2). We were then able to get each of the key people to plan out the action steps needed to make the re-launch work. We were keen to avoid being a one-hit wonder, with one bang and then a whimper, a problem Shelly said she had with most of her boyfriends.

The end of the year was critical for us, as we had to get our re-launch off to a flying start. We thought a good event to tap into was Boxing Day, and we would try to be its unofficial sponsor. We thought that most families ate together on the 25th December itself, a day hundreds of brands wanted to be associated with. But we would try to keep the festive family spirit alive the day after Xmas and beyond. In the New Year we'd keep the campaign for family eating going with the Simpton's

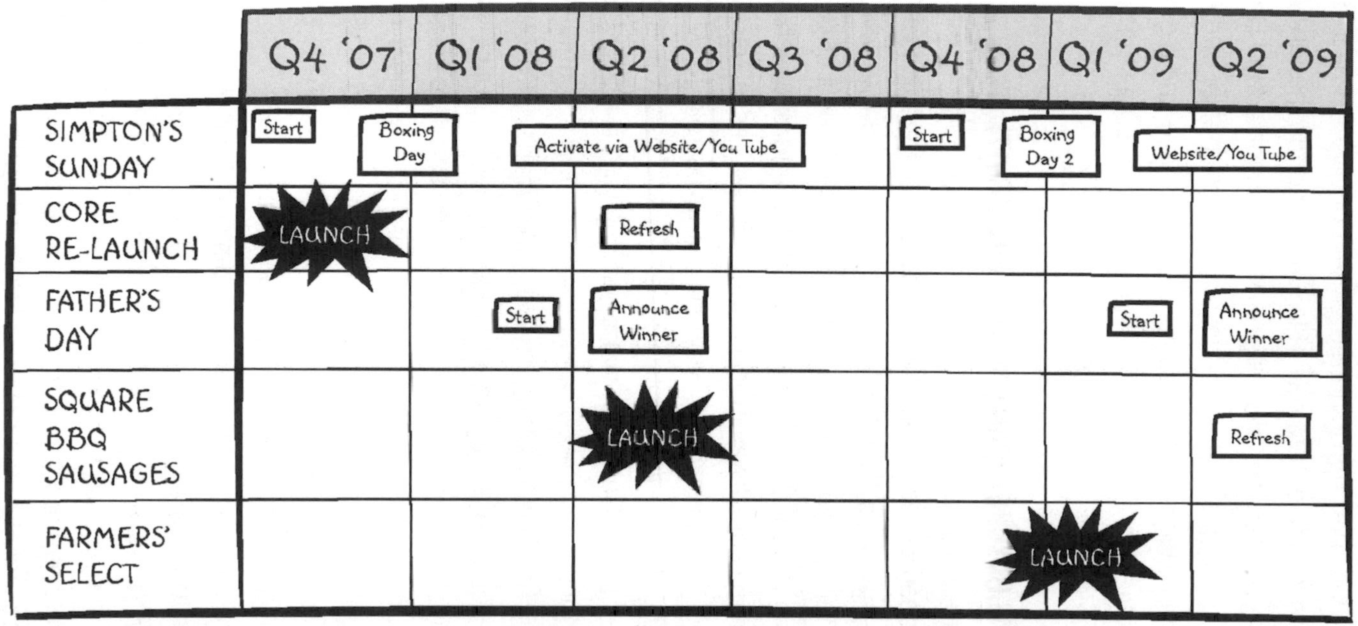

	Q4 '07	Q1 '08	Q2 '08	Q3 '08	Q4 '08	Q1 '09	Q2 '09
SIMPTON'S SUNDAY	Start	Boxing Day	Activate via Website/You Tube		Start	Boxing Day 2	Website/You Tube
CORE RE-LAUNCH	LAUNCH		Refresh				
FATHER'S DAY		Start	Announce Winner			Start	Announce Winner
SQUARE BBQ SAUSAGES			LAUNCH				Refresh
FARMERS' SELECT						LAUNCH	

Figure 8.2: 'Episodic' marketing plan

Sunday idea. We then planned a second big event to tie in with Father's Day on Sunday 18th June and the launch of the square sausages. We would ask kids to nominate their Dad as the best barbequer in the country, and offer special barbeque kits for the 20 winners. In this way we would have one big event in the winter, and another in the summer. We would keep wave after wave of news coming on the brand.

HUGO THE HATCHET MAN (FRIDAY, AUGUST 17)

I now have a suspicion about the reason for Hugo's smug expression earlier this month. I was called into the office of Andy Nichols, the Sales Director, the first meeting I'd had with him all year. Without so much as a bit of small-talk or a chocolate biscuit, he dropped his bomb-shell, the sound of which is still ringing in my ears. I was going back to Sales. Tessa was being promoted to a prestigious new global sales role to work on distributing our products outside the UK. And he wanted me to fill her old job in Category Management, with a special focus on, you guessed it, the pizza launch. I was now sure that Tessa and Hugo had been plotting my downfall when I spied on them at Soho House. After all, this move would get me out of Hugo's hair at last, allowing him to wind down the sausage marketing plan *and* force me to help make his pet pizza project work. I light-heartedly asked Andy if Hugo had put him up to this. My suspicions were confirmed when instead of laughing off the question, Andy nervously inspected his shoes.

He changed the subject, assuring me that this was not only a chance to boost my salary by 20%, it was my best chance of challenging Tessa for the Sales Director's job in the New Year. If I didn't move back to Sales now, then he couldn't guarantee what would happen to me, which I took as a thinly veiled threat that I'd be looking for a new job. When I said I'd think about it, he laughed nervously, assuming I was joking. But I wasn't. I'd already been tempted once, by the Tesco job, and decided to stay. And having now sold our sausage plans, although in scaled-down form, I was even less keen to quit. The meeting ended awkwardly, like a couple where the guy had asked his girlfriend to marry him, only to have her say she'd think it over. Andy urged me to think fast, as he'd have to look outside the company if I didn't want the job.

Not surprisingly, when I told Claire the news about the chance to go back to Sales she couldn't understand why I hadn't bitten off not one but both of Andy's arms. After all, the Sales Director's job *was* the one I'd always dreamt of having. When I told her about my suspicion that Hugo had a hand in the affair, she scolded me for reading too many detective novels. I also think that Claire would secretly be glad to see me back with the boys in Sales, rather than spending all my days and too many nights with Jane.

Well, I have a couple of weeks on holiday in Tuscany to think things over. Can I really turn down a second chance to move back into Sales, this one on an even more attractive silver platter?

AUGUST'S SUMMARY

1. Have a point of view before you do research so you can develop your own intuition.
2. Bringing to life insight with video is much more effective than a PowerPoint presentation.
3. Vision is one thing, but you also need to work with the team on the action plan to make it come to life.
4. A brand plan needs several waves or 'episodes' of activity.

9.

September – Don't just think different, *do* different (the importance of execution)

RAINING ON THE PIZZA PARADE (TUESDAY, SEPTEMBER 4)

Back from holiday feeling refreshed and revived, even if I'm still unsure on what to do about the move back to Sales. Andy's reluctantly given me another couple of weeks to decide. Hugo for one looks happier than I've seen him in a long time; he's probably sure he's about to get rid of me.

I forced thoughts of the job situation to the back of my mind, as we needed to crack on with the detailed execution of our sausage plan. The further down the track I could get, the less chance Hugo had of scuppering things if I did leave. The first and most important thing to work on was the product, so Jane and I made another trip up to the factory today to check how Ron and the team were getting on with the new sausage production. We took up a boot full of pizza samples to try out with the team, in the same way we had done with the new sausages.

Even though I wasn't a big fan of the product launch, I thought it was important that the team had a chance to try it before they saw it on the supermarket shelves. We offered Hugo the chance to come with us, but he declined. He was even less interested in what a bunch of factory workers had to say about his 'masterpiece' than he was in the opinion of consumers. And anyway, he had an important meeting with Kitty, the planner from ETC. Jane pointed out that Hugo seemed to spend most of his time these days in meetings with Kitty, which was curious seeing as how most of her work on the new pizza campaign had been done.

Unsurprisingly, the pizza-tasting session at the factory was a bit of a washout, especially compared with the enthusiastic response we got from the sausage-tasting session we did last month. Wandering around and listening in on people's conversations confirmed my fears about the product not offering anything new compared with the retailers' own ones. They looked the same, had the same ingredients, and tasted the same. Which was no surprise seeing as how they were made in the same factory on the same production line. And when people heard how much the pizzas would cost they almost choked on their chorizo. Jane's half-hearted attempts to vaunt the appeal of the limited edition designer boxes failed to fan even faint flames of enthusiasm.

By the time we finished it was already 7pm, and with torrential rain making the M6 motorway even less attractive than normal, we decided to stay at the local Holiday Inn, and drive back early in the morning. As we walked to the car Jane shook her head, saying that today was the final confirmation that the pizza launch was doomed to failure. Now she could really see the error of relying solely on the concept of a lifestyle pizza to differentiate us. We had been *thinking* differently about the sort of brand we wanted, but not *doing* enough to really deliver.

IN THE DOG-HOUSE (WEDNESDAY, SEPTEMBER 5)

Jane and I drove back South this morning in stony silence after the painfully embarrassing events of last night. As a result of what happened, Claire has said I come back home having accepted the sales job, or I don't come home at all.

I blame the three bottles of red wine and the double Cointreau nightcap Jane and I used to drown our pizza troubles. After stumbling back to my room at midnight I'd taken a cold shower to try and freshen up, only to be interrupted by a knock at the door. I opened the door to find Jane, wrapped only in a towel, her eyes red with tears. I asked her in and she slumped down on the bed, explaining between sobs that her boyfriend had just dumped her by text. I knew from what she'd told me earlier that the guy in question was an old flame who lived in her home town, not far from the factory. He wanted her to move back up North, disliking what he saw as her snobby Southern lifestyle.

I sat next to her and reluctantly put my arm round her to provide some comfort, which in retrospect sent the wrong signals. Jane turned her head to me, and before I knew it she was kissing me. I broke off the kiss, a little too slowly for comfort, and jumped off the bed, heading to the bathroom to escape and locking the door behind me. And that's when it all went horribly wrong. The phone rang, and before I could get out I heard Jane explaining that I was busy in the bathroom. I didn't need to ask who the caller was: the look of horror on Jane's face told me it was Claire.

Jane was doubly upset about the whole thing. First, because of the damage to my relationship with Claire. But she was also horrified to hear that this meant I would have to go back to Sales early, leaving her and Brian with Hugo as a boss again.

THE DEVIL IS IN THE DETAIL (FRIDAY, SEPTEMBER 7)

I was allowed back in the house, even though I hadn't accepted the sales job, but was banished to the spare room. I blamed my delay in accepting the offer on Andy being out of town for a week at a sales conference in Portugal. In the meantime, I just want to plough ahead and get as far as I can on our sausage plans.

Got some great inspiration from a webcast I watched today about a guy called Robert Stephens, the Founder and 'Chief Inspector' of US-based computer repair company The Geek Squad. The name and logo were inspired by 1960s TV cop shows like Dragnet and Police Squad. The name was chosen to sound more like a movie than a standard repair company and to make his business sound bigger than it really was. His US-based computer repair company has grown from a one-man start-up to a company employing 15 000 'agents' in the USA, with a UK launch planned with Carphone Warehouse. And all this without the need for advertising. As I listened intently to the presentation I found myself nodding like one of those toy dogs you used to see in the back of car windows.

First of all, Stephens pointed out that the foundation of his company's success was a great product and he had a brilliant quote that I look forward to sharing with Kitty from ETC: 'Advertising is a tax for having an unremarkable product'! This started with him looking at each step of the computer repair experience and highlighting numerous ways to make it better, such as explaining repairs in language people understood and arriving 5 minutes early for his appointment. Not rocket science, but doing the basics better than the competition in lots of areas, that together created differentiation. New features have also been added over time, including a service guarantee, flat rates to remove the discomfort of billing by the hour and not using third-party repairers.

The most interesting thing about the brand was the way Stephens **designed every single bit of the Geek Squad experience to create word-of-mouth** (wheresthesausage. com). He'd been forced to do this because of the lack of money for conventional advertising and went as far as urging the people in the audience to cut their own budgets if they wanted to be truly creative. I laughed to myself as I thought that I was actually doing something leading edge, even though my budget cut had been forced on me by Hugo blowing all the budget on his pizza project. At the heart of his business were the 'agents' with their unforgettable uniforms, black clip-on ties (to stop you being strangled by nasty printers) and Geek Squad badges. The Geek Squad cars were also designed to get noticed, with vintage cars at the start and now VW Beetles.

But my favourite bit of differentiation was the shoes. He was told that with 15 000 agents the company could get a free logo on the side of them. Instead, he asked for a reversed-out logo on the soles. Why? Because this meant branded footprints everywhere his agents go. Think about it. 30 000 shoes, 100 steps a day... makes 3 million free adverts!

The distinctive tone and style was also translated into a brand language that communicates efficiency but with an amusing twist. You're confident the job will get done, but entertained at the same time. For example, the company's employees are described as 'an elite tactical unit of highly trained Agents that focus solely on computer and network support'. And the Geek Squad units inside computer retailer Best Buy are christened 'precincts'.

I finished the webcast feeling fired up. After all, if The Geek Squad could differentiate something as banal and boring as computer repairs, surely we could do the same with our sausages? I made a mental note to ask the team to collect their own examples of brands that had successfully stood out from the crowd.

PIZZA PROBLEMS (MONDAY, SEPTEMBER 17)

Seems like our guinea pigs at the factory are not the only ones complaining about the lack of differentiation in our pizzas. I had lunch today with John from Sales and he told me that the reaction from our retail customers was underwhelming to say the least. There were rumblings that some of the retailers would cut back the shelf-space that our pizza would get.

The supermarkets had agreed to list the product almost a year ago based on an over-the-top sales pitch from Hugo, including the promise of a multi-million pound blockbuster advertising campaign starring Kate Moss. With the product due on the shelves by the end of the month, the reality of the launch was of course not quite as spectacular, and Z-list Brandy was not quite in the same league as Ms Moss. The only thing that did look like a supermodel was the super-thin advertising budget, slimmed down to cover the volume shortfall on our sausage business.

I bumped into Hugo on the way back from the coffee machine and when I mentioned the threat of reduced shelf-space I was surprised that he looked genuinely concerned. However, his concern was not to do with the risk of reduced sales, but rather a fear of not being able to display all five limited edition packs together, meaning his Pizzart wall would be a brick or two shorter than what he had hoped for. He then went on to tell me with a grin that I would soon be in charge of sorting out his display problems for him. It was all I could do to stop myself from head-butting the smarmy bugger.

DIFFERENTIATION DAY (THURSDAY, SEPTEMBER 20)

Today we had a great meeting to share our examples of brands that had succeeded in being different in their execution. After going through all of these, we grouped the resulting ideas into three main areas. The first of these was product features and ingredients. Shelly had brought along her Pantene with Pro-Vitamin B5 and we all agreed that her hair was looking especially shiny as a result of using it. I didn't have the heart to say that it would have looked even better if the dark roots hadn't been showing. On the Simpton's side we agreed to make as much as we could out of our original 'secret' recipe that was, like Coca-Cola's, locked away in a safe.

The second area was the use of music and other brand 'properties' in communication. Jane showed us an example of the communication used by cat-food brand Felix, which featured a cartoon cat of the same name. The endline used was 'Cats like Felix like Felix'. Jane told us that **Felix had been able to take market leadership from the Whiskas brand whilst spending only half the amount of money** (wheresthesausage.com). The consistent use of the same character helped them to get much more bang for their buck. We agreed to look at how we could create a communication property of our own to help us stand out from the crowd.

The most exciting area of all though was the third and last one, to do with packaging. The meeting room table was full of fantastic packaging examples we had brought in. Sticking with the animal theme, Jane had brought a packet of Andrex toilet tissue, which had used the same puppy on it for ages. This helped communicate the brand idea of being 'soft and strong', in addition to helping them stand out on the shelf. And Brian chipped in with a couple of jars of barbeque sauce he had seen when on a stag weekend in Amsterdam, from a Dutch brand called Calve. **They had created two special edition versions each with their own distinctive pack designs and products** (wheresthesausage.com). Barbeque Beast was a hot and spicy product with a leopard-skin wrapper, and Barbeque Beauty was a mild and fruity sauce with a flowery pack design We all thought these sort of packs would 'jump' off the shelf, and also be practically impossible for own label brands to copy. Jane offered to follow up with Ron about doing limited edition special packs like these for our own barbeque promotion we were planning for next summer.

Over dinner Claire reminded me that my week was up, and that on Monday I needed to tell Andy I was going back to Sales. Or else.

BRIAN'S BRAVERY SAVES THE DAY (FRIDAY, SEPTEMBER 21)

Ended the week on a real low, and left the office in a glum mood, as it was probably my last day in brand management. Jane and Brian had left early, so I couldn't even say my last goodbye.

Arrived home ready to tell Claire that I was going to accept Andy's offer, only to find her deep in conversation with none other than Jane and Brian. I was left completely confused when Claire jumped up and gave me the first hug I'd had in a week, and the biggest kiss I'd had in much longer. When I asked for an explanation, she pointed at Brian, who was beaming proudly and waving a piece of paper. He handed me the paper, which turned out to be a print-out of an email from Hugo to Jonathon Simpton. As I read it, the expletives I emitted about my boss got louder and ruder. The email proved that Hugo had indeed set me up. In it he thanked the company's CEO for having agreed to his request to put pressure on Andy Nichols to promote Tessa into a new role her place. Hugo also mentioned that he agreed with the decision to give Tessa the Sales Director's job in January. I knew Tessa and Hugo were up to no good, but did this mean Andy was also in on things? Even if I had accepted the move back to Sales, I was never in line for his job.

When I asked Brian how he'd got hold of the email he grinned and explained that Hugo should change the password on his PC to something other than 'password'. Claire apologized for having dismissed my suspicions about Hugo's dirty deeds, and said she was so proud that my prospects in marketing were so bright. I was about to ask where this sudden and totally misinformed optimism about my future in brand management had come from when I saw Jane wink slyly at me.

In addition to finding out the truth about Hugo's dirty deeds, the other bit of good news was that Jane had given a heartfelt apology to Claire about what had happened in the Holiday Inn. She explained that I was completely innocent, with her claims helped by the rather large engagement ring she was wearing.

SEPTEMBER'S SUMMARY

1. Differentiation is a combination of smart strategy and excellent execution.
2. You need to look at loads of different opportunities for differentiation, not just one, such as packaging design, promotions, sampling and the product itself.
3. Having little or even no funds for conventional marketing can be a great stimulus for creativity, forcing you to inject the brand idea into everything you do.

Quarter Four

THE RUBBER HITS THE ROAD (AS THE PIZZA HITS THE FAN)

10.

October – Rallying the troops (beyond 'brand-washing' to true engagement)

BRAND-WASHING (MONDAY, OCTOBER 8)

Took great pleasure in telling Hugo last week that I wouldn't be taking the job in Sales after all, and watching his eyes bulge out of their sockets in shock and horror. He told me he'd make me regret my decision, and he spent today doing his best to live up to his promise.

We spent the day at the ETC offices in Soho for a briefing on the presentations for the annual brand conference that happens every October. This brings together 200 people from all the different departments (Sales, HR, Production, etc.) to see the marketing plans for the following year. Hugo announced that the pizza launch would of course take up most of the day, and get all the production budget. He announced dismissively that I would have half an hour at the end to talk about my plans, as if he was tossing a few scraps to the family dog under the table.

Hugo and Kitty explained that the event was part of their plan to 'engage' our employees with the Simpton's mission and inspire them to 'live the brand'. I'm a big believer in getting people fired up about working on your brand but, not surprisingly, I disagree with the way Hugo wants to do this. He summed up his approach as 'putting the show into business'. It seems to involve blowing a huge budget on flashy presentations that talked *at* people.

Kitty showed us an artist's impression of the stage and lighting for the event at the Carling Apollo in Hammersmith that did indeed look more like a rock concert than a sausage conference. The backdrop was a huge screen with the graffiti-based design for the pizza box that Hugo had crowned the Grand Prix from the five entries in the competition.

At the end of the presentation Kitty handed Hugo a Simpton's baseball cap that he placed on his head and then twisted round backwards with a flourish. To our horror he then launched into a rap:

Now I'm a man on a sausage mission
It's tough out there, a war of attrition
Take no prisoners, give no ground
Gotta build the business, pound by pound

We used to be a sausage brand, nothing more
But now we gotta a whole new way to score
Movin' ahead, keepin' up with the times
Listen to my rap, you'll see it chimes

It's round, it's thick and it's pipin' hot
It'll move your world, I kid you not
It's gonna take the supermarkets by storm
It's a pizza party that will last till dawn

Let me hear ya all shout 'Simpton's Pizza'!
From the home of the leaning tower of Pisa
We'll take it, bake it and bring it to the street
It's a brand movin' forward to the hip-hop beat

The end of Hugo's rap was met with rapturous applause from Kitty and her two side-kicks, who were both on their feet. Jane leant over and whispered that it was more David Brent than 50 Cent.

The rest of the day was taken up by Hugo's mind-numbing presentation on his vision for the Simpton's brand. It was a Greatest Hits compilation of all the jargon, buzzwords and complicated diagrams from the year so far. The page numbers on the bottom right-hand corner of the screen started to blur after a while, but I think the total was over 300 pages in all.

By the end of the day I felt like I'd suffered 'death by Power-Point', with my brain turned into a big dollop of mashed potato. I stumbled through the font door mumbling incoherently and scared the children. Amy ran tearfully Into the kitchen, explaining between sobs that I was talking like one of the intensive care patients from Casualty with wires and tubes plugged in them. After a large gin and tonic had partially resuscitated me, I talked Claire through the day's events. The problem was that Hugo's presentation was just that, a presentation. It was heavy on words, but light on action. He was preaching his Simpsational gospel, but when it came to what the brand was going to do, all we had was our me-too pizza. Also, apart from the rap, the actual presentation was far from Simpsational, it was a 300-page PowerPoint chart-fest. Hugo was asking our people to do one thing, and then doing the opposite himself.

But what could I do that was better, especially seeing as how I had only half an hour and no budget. It did seem that Hugo had done a good job of stitching me up. And if the presentation was a flop, it could harm the chances of getting the support of the people in the company that we desperately needed.

LEADING FROM THE FRONT (MONDAY, OCTOBER 15)

Inspiration for my spot at the brand conference came today from one of my heroes, Steve Jobs, the CEO of Apple. I'm a signed-up member of iPodaholics anonymous, buying every new model that comes out, even though the old one is perfectly fine, which drives Claire mad (it seems that the rule of pointless duplication applies to boys' toys, but not shoes and handbags). The latest iPod video with a full screen arrived in the post today and I spent most of the morning setting it up and linking it to my beautiful iMac computer. When I went on the Apple website to download the latest episode of Top Gear, I noticed a headline about Steve Jobs' most recent presentation at MacExpo, the annual Apple event where they launch their new product range. This could not have been further away from Hugo's PowerPoint-heavy presentation. Jobs' approach was all about the design and functionality of the products. He didn't *tell* people that Apple was innovative; he *showed* them innovative products. He didn't use wordy charts (or dodgy raps) to communicate that Apple was cool; he had pop stars like Madonna and Bono on stage with their own iPods singing the praises of the product. The other thing that struck me was how sincere and genuine Jobs was in his love of the brand, and how passionate he was about the product. He was like a kid who had just opened a sack full of amazing presents from Santa on Xmas morning, bursting with enthusiasm to show off his new toys. **There were no brand pyramids in sight, but boy did you have a crystal clear idea of what Apple stood for** (wheresthesausage.com).

PEOPLE AT PRET (TUESDAY, OCTOBER 16)

Got some more clues on how to get people excited about the Simpton's brand from a trip to Pret à Manger this lunchtime. I've always been impressed by the way that the people working there seem to always be polite and smiley. This is a welcome contrast to the glum-looking, surly teenagers who serve me when the magnetic pull of the latest McDonald's Happy Meal toy is too strong to fight off. I could see from the badge of the person serving me that he was the manager of the store, so I asked if I could quiz him about how he kept his staff so motivated. He agreed to talk if I could hang around for an hour or so, as he was helping out during the rush hour. This reply was interesting in itself: when the store was busy he rolled up his sleeves, rather than sitting in his office drinking coffee.

The chat we had later was fascinating. I started by asking if an engagement programme had been used to help get the staff to live the brand. His face looked like mine must do when I'm listening to Hugo's brand-babble, and he asked if I could repeat the question in English. I explained I was interested in **how Pret got their people to consistently deliver great service** (wheresthesausage.com). This time he smiled and said there were four simple things that all seemed basic, but as is often the case in life, doing the basics really well seems to be quite hard:

1. *Right product*: people are proud of the sandwiches they make fresh each morning, using only natural and high-quality ingredients. Any sandwiches left at the end of the day are given to charity.
2. *Right people*: many of the staff are well-educated international students. All candidates work in a store for a day, and existing staff members vote on whether to offer them a job.

3. *Right reward*: people are paid 20% more than the competition and staff who get a positive mention from a customer get a solid silver star made by Tiffany & Co. Also, 75% of store managers started working in a store, so the chances for promotion are quite good.
4. *Right leaders*: store managers treat people with respect and, as I had seen for myself, led by example. Rather than shouting at staff to give good service, they modelled the right behaviour, and helped out when it got busy.

The manager excused himself as he needed to help clean up, leaving me to jot down Pret's four steps to success on a brown paper bag (Figure 10.1). The one about hiring people reminded me of what I had learnt about Nike, who only hired sports enthusiasts. Shouldn't we be hiring people who were into food and cooking? The rewards point was also relevant. From what I had seen at Simpton's there were no clear measures of brand success, and so no link between brand performance and people's rewards. And the point on product pride was perhaps the

Figure 10.1: Beyond brand-washing

most important of all. The best way to get people engaged with the brand was surely to start making and selling products again that we all felt proud about.

LEADING FROM THE FRONT (WEDNESDAY, OCTOBER 24)

Just back from the brand event. Hugo's performance in the morning was greeted with roars of laughter, with people laughing at him rather than with him. I would almost have felt sorry for him humiliating himself if it wasn't for the way he took it all so seriously. He stormed off the stage in a huff at the end of the rap, and had to be cajoled to come back and do his brand presentation. If the lights hadn't been turned up bright for this bit, Hugo's PowerPoint-fest would have been drowned out by 200 people snoring.

My session started just before lunchtime, by which point people were getting very restless and you could almost hear the stomachs rumbling. My introduction announcing 20 minutes of PowerPoint-free presentation followed by lunch was greeted with the first real applause of the day. The only person who looked less than happy was Hugo. I told a simple story from the heart about my dream of making Simpton's proud again about its sausages, and how we needed to rediscover what made us famous but make it relevant for today with the 'Real taste of home' idea. I showed a compilation of James Bond movie clips to make this point. Jane came on and revealed our Simpton's Sunday campaign idea and we then showed the video that was our finale. We had discovered that Brian was something of a budding film director, or at least a You Tube video director. And to illustrate the campaign idea he had secretly filmed the kids of ten of the key people in the audience talking about family meals, or rather the lack of them. The sight of little boys and girls asking their Mums and Dads to at least have one day a week when they cooked a meal for them tugged at the heartstrings. I could even see one of the most hardened sales guys having to wipe his eyes and blame the dust in the room when he saw his kids on film. By this point the three of us felt we had the audience in the palm of our hands. I myself was worryingly starting to feel like Robbie Williams, and so it was perfect timing for Ron to come on stage and introduce the new products we wanted to launch. OK, square-shaped sausages are not as sexy as the new iPod, but 200 hungry people were happy to tuck into the samples that were waiting in the café next to the concert hall.

As people enjoyed their lunch I walked through the café keen to eavesdrop on conversations about the morning. I was pleased to see that almost everyone was talking about our sausage presentation, in between imitating Hugo's embarrassing attempts at rapping. Several people stopped me to say thanks for such an inspiring and refreshing presentation, and to enthuse about the new sausage products they had sampled. The other thing I heard a lot of was whispers of discontent about the pizza launch. It seems that a couple of the biggest supermarket chains had put the pizza into only their top 50 stores to see how sales went, before rolling it out to the rest. And based on the early signals, there was a real risk that this wouldn't happen.

I had hoped to have a word with Andy Nichols, to persuade him that I should still be given a crack at the Sales Director's job. Unfortunately he left, locked deep in conversation with the person who it looks like he's already picked, Tessa Williams.

VIDEO KILLED THE SAUSAGE STAR (MONDAY, OCTOBER 29)

Well, **Hugo's performance at the brand event has got a reaction bigger than he could ever have hoped for** (wheresthesausage.com), though not the one he had in mind. It seems that someone used their brand new pink phone camera to catch Hugo in all his glory. The video has made its way onto You Tube, and so far has been seen by an amazing 20 000 people. This might explain why Hugo has been off work for the last couple of days suffering from some sort of mystery illness.

OCTOBER'S SUMMARY

1. Brand engagement starts with having a product or service people feel proud to work on.
2. Brand engagement that relies only on communication is really brand-washing.
3. The best way to inspire people is to lead by example: they will doubt what you say, but believe what you do.
4. What gets measured gets done: reward the sort of behaviour you want on the brand.

11.

November – Making money, not movies (communication should tell a product story)

SPONSORED ENTERTAINMENT (MONDAY, NOVEMBER 5)

We need to get cracking on communication this month, to be ready for the festive season. However, we were struggling to get any attention from ETC as they were apparently still finishing off the pizza advertising. This morning we got to see the fruits of their labour at the 'premiere' of the commercial.

Hugo and Kitty from ETC had hired a private cinema at a swanky hotel called St Martins Lane, with huge blue leather armchairs and little tables to rest your cappuccino on. It certainly made a change from my normal cinema trip to the local popcorn-ridden Odeon. Shelly, Brian, Jane and I found the last few seats free on the back row, with the other 30 or so places taken by people from the ad agency and production company. Before the advert itself we had to sit through a 30-minute 'the making of' film that Hugo was hoping would be picked up by a TV station. The chances of this happening were always slim, and now wafer thin, given that Kate Moss had been replaced by Brandy. And I'm not sure how many people will want to watch 30 minutes of Hugo hanging out with the film's director musing on the creative interpretation of his pizza vision.

The commercial was beautiful to look at, but then it did cost a mind-boggling million pounds to shoot it. It had been made in Monte Carlo, and showed Brandy living the millionairess life-style. The script was pretty much the same as the one we'd seen a couple of months ago. We saw her wining and dining at the swanky Hotel de Paris and then zooming off in a Ferrari to dance till dawn. She rounded the evening off with a slice of Simpton's pizza served by a small army of muscle-bound waiters, all naked from the waist up. Shelly reliably informed us that Hugo had done the casting for these roles himself, taking a full week to get just the right actors. The problem with the commercial was that if you blinked for a second at the end of it you wouldn't have the foggiest idea that it was for Simpton's pizza. If you did have to guess what it was for you were more likely to say champagne or perfume than sausage pizza. It was a beautiful 30-second mini-movie, paid for by Simpton's, or 'sponsored entertainment' as Jane aptly put it.

When the lights came up, the audience burst into rapturous applause and jumped to their feet. Kitty from ETC made an im-passioned speech about how Hugo was a true visionary before presenting him and the film's director with a bottle of vintage cham-pagne. The thing that struck me as strange was the way the pizza launch campaign was based so heavily on TV. I'd been reading a book called 'The death of the 30-second spot' that Jane recom-mended to me, and it showed the dramatic decline of TV and the rise of the internet. ETC and Hugo seemed stuck in the past where the agency said 'The answer's TV. What's the question?'

THE PIZZA HITS THE FAN (WEDNESDAY, NOVEMBER 7)

I arrived in the office a bit late this morning as I made the mistake of dropping the kids off at school in the car, and got caught in the 4x4 jam. I noticed that Old Mr Simpton's Bentley was parked outside reception. Little did I know how ominous a sign this was.

When I arrived I saw Shelly, Jane and Brian huddled together in deep conversation, with worried looks on their faces. I assumed they were talking about the latest boyfriend that Shelly had dumped, but the truth was closer to home. Jane had been out with a friend who worked in Sales and had learnt that the whispers of discontent about the pizza launch had turned into a deafening chorus of complaints. The TV advertising was yet to start, but even without it we should have been seeing much better sales. The product was sitting on the shelf like a sulking toddler, refusing to budge. As a result, we were entering the 'death spiral': poor sales leading to reduced space on the shelf, leading to less visibility, leading to even worse sales and so on. The rumour was that Tesco were about to de-list us, which would pull the plug out of the life-support machine of our critically ill pizza launch. I could hear the sickening hum of the flat-lining heart monitor now.

Our conversation was interrupted by Hugo striding straight past us, head down and upper body leaning forward, looking like one of the power-walkers I see in the park. He marched into his office and slammed the door so hard that a framed picture of Brandy fell to the floor with a shattering of glass. We looked at each other for a few seconds until the others nudged me in the direction of Hugo. Reluctantly I tiptoed towards his office, and peered inside to see our boss sitting at his desk with his head in his hands. I knocked gently on the door and when Hugo looked up I could have sworn his eyes were red from crying. His only response was to put his head back in his hands, and I took this as permission to enter. After several attempts to get him to explain what had happened, he finally mumbled that his masterpiece would never be on the screen. Old Mr Simpton had cut the budget for the TV advertising to protect the profit for the year, effectively driving a stake into the heart of the pizza launch. Sales were already bad, and with the removal of the TV advertising cavalry coming over the hill, the product launch was doomed.

I left Hugo to mourn the death of his pizza campaign, shocked that he was more worried about not seeing his advert on TV than he was about the impact on the business. He seemed to have forgotten he was here to make money, not movies. I went back to my desk to find none other than Old Mr Simpton sat in my chair. He explained glumly that he had never believed in the pizza launch from the start, but had given his nephew and Hugo the benefit of the doubt. After all, they were young and supposedly better educated in the ways of 21st century marketing. It turns out that the world may have changed a lot, but good old-fashioned common sense would never go out of fashion. He had indeed chopped the pizza launch budget and the good news was that he was giving us some of it to turn our regional sausage re-launch into a national event. He stood up and solemnly explained that the future of the business was now in our hands. The negative fallout from the failed pizza launch was going to hit the headlines soon, and the vultures would start circling straight after. Private equity investors had been calling him daily in an attempt to buy the business, and although he didn't want to sell, he had an increasingly hard job to keep the support of the other family shareholders. No pressure then.

TIGHTER BRIEFS ARE BETTER (MONDAY, NOVEMBER 12)

I'm determined to avoid making the same mistakes as Hugo when developing the communication for our sausage re-launch. We mustn't make another piece of sponsored entertainment, needing to do a much better job of selling the product to drive sales. And to do this we needed a tighter brief for what we were trying to do.

I got some welcome inspiration from a Marks & Spencer's chocolate pudding advert Claire and I saw on Saturday night. In contrast to our pizza ad, the second this one started I knew which brand it was for. I recognized the music, although it was almost drowned out by the moans and groans that Claire was making next to me on the sofa. Her reaction was understandable, as the chocolate pudding in question did look amazing. The film did a great job of celebrating the product, taking time to show a fork appearing and then piercing the pud, with a river of steaming sauce pouring out. The languorous voice-over then told us that 'This isn't just food. It's M&S food'. It was more than that even; it was food porn.

The effectiveness of the commercial was confirmed in two ways the following day. First, when we sat down to dinner after the kids had finally gone to bed we had M&S chocolate pud for dessert. Second, and more importantly, a quick bit of Googling led me to news of the Advertising Effectiveness Awards. **M&S and their agency had won the Grand Prix for their work, which had played a major role in the brand's turnaround** (wheresthesausage.com). Claire had not been the only person to rush out and purchase the puds: sales had increased by a whopping 288%! I loved the quote made by the editor of advertising magazine *Campaign*: 'These ads haven't troubled creative juries much. But they've sold puddings, pants and party dresses. Job done, and sod what the creative cliques think.'

The M&S advertising did have some emotional sizzle and sex appeal, but this was focused on dramatizing the product. This was also the same approach I had heard earlier in the year from the Dove lady at the brand conference. They had tried to do commercials that talked about the brand's philosophy and beliefs, called their 'beauty theory', but these had failed to move their consumers. Success came when they took a product story, about the firming range that had been 'tested on real curves', and 'wrapped this in beauty theory'. The learning was the same: tell a product story in an entertaining and memorable way.

I spent the afternoon working with Jane on a communication brief for the agency. We started by clarifying the job to be done and took inspiration from Lynx's 'Spray more, get more' campaign that had prompted me to buy a boxed set for my nephew earlier in the year. Through a friend, Jane had met the Lynx brand manager who worked on this campaign and got the inside story. The global brand team had looked at why sales of the brand in Argentina were much higher than in Brazil. The answer was use of the spray not just under the arms, but all over the upper body (and some bits below as well). This led to a communication brief with a clear job: get boys to spray it all over.

When we discussed our brief, we decided the key job was to get some of the many people who'd deserted our brand for own label sausages to come back and try us again. We figured these people would be easier to attract than people who had never heard of us. We had to be focused, owing to the limited budget we had to spend. The second question was which bit of the brand positioning we wanted to concentrate on. We wanted to avoid the 'kitchen sink' mistake of asking the poor agency to get across a shopping list of messages. Again, we had to focus.

We highlighted 'rediscover the taste of home' as our main idea, supported by the return to our original recipe. This felt like it had potential, as there was a common theme of 'home-coming' that worked at several levels. The idea was rooted in the product, as we were coming home to *our* roots with an improved product by going back to the original recipe. And our old users were coming back to enjoy the taste they re-membered. On the emotional side, we wanted to encourage the family to eat together again and rediscover the pleasure of home-cooked food. It did feel like we were telling a product story, but in an emotionally appealing way. We finished the brief by emphasizing the need to create a communication idea that would work across different channels, and suggested that a non-TV approach was likely to be the way to go.

OUR TUBE (WEDNESDAY, NOVEMBER 14)

I was due to brief ETC today on our re-launch communication, but they didn't come in. In fact, they won't be coming in any more at all. We had been using the old school way of paying our agencies based on a percentage commission of the me-dia spend. With the TV budget slashed, their fee was about to go the same way, and would not be enough to keep them in the style they were accustomed to. It was actually a bit of a relief to not have to work with Kitty and her crew, as I had seri-ous doubts about their ability to create communication aimed at selling sausages rather than seducing the juries of creative awards ceremonies. However, this did mean we were stuck without an agency to help us. I put a call in to the small agency called Zebra who had helped us when we were exploring brand ideas, and prayed that they had time to help us out.

While I waited for them to call back, I spent an hour with Brian to look at some ideas he had come up with to help promote Simpton's Sunday campaign. His idea was to shoot a series of short films with a lady called Laura we'd met during our research into family eating habits. She was a specialist in family relationships with a passion for the role played by food and eating habits. Brian's idea was for him to shoot a series of mini-movies that would show Laura sharing tips on how to get the family eating together round the table again at least once a week. The great thing about the proposal was that it would be free to shoot and to air.

The other key task of the day was checking in with Ron at the factory to see how they were coping with the huge jump in production needed to allow us to do a national re-launch, not just a regional one. The production challenge was big, but it was heart-warming to hear how loads of local people had agreed to work part-time on extra shifts to meet demand. The whole community was behind our re-launch as they saw it as a way to make a last stand to save the factory. They, more than anyone, feared the prospect of the company being gobbled up in a predatory take-over.

SIMPTON'S IS COMING HOME (THURSDAY, NOVEMBER 22)

Zebra came in to see us today, and what a job they have done. In just one week they have come up with an idea that I think might just save our bacon and sausage. They said the clear brief and the videos we gave them from our immersion visits had been a big help.

They had picked up our unofficial sponsorship of Boxing Day, and wanted to link this with the brand idea of coming home. They suggested focusing on the angle of people coming back to spend the festive season with their families. Radio adverts would be used to create brand awareness during the lead up to Xmas. In addition, a creative use of press advertising involved mini-adverts in the Boxing Day schedules of TV listing pages. Each ad would be like someone had drawn a red ring around part of the schedule, but rather than a programme, this would be a reminder to stock up on Simpton's to make Boxing Day go with a bang.

But the agency hadn't finished, and ended with a bang themselves. They proposed a TV part of the plan, at which point I was about to protest. But they quickly moved on and their idea halted my complaints in their tracks. The idea was risky, but if it comes off it will be brilliant. The idea is to ask real families to video themselves enjoying their Simpton's Boxing Day homecoming and upload these to our website. We would edit them into a series of 10-second films in the afternoon, and then air the resulting commercials in the evening. Each TV region would see a film of someone from a local town. It was a long shot, but it felt like it might just be a big enough idea to help save the sausage business.

NOVEMBER'S SUMMARY

1. Communication that has only emotional sizzle and no product sausage is 'sponsored entertainment'.
2. Marketing people (apart from Hugo) are here to make money, not movies.
3. The most effective communication tells a product story in an interesting way.
4. TV is not always the answer and should never be the place to start. We need a big brand idea that can then be translated into different media.

12.

December – The sausage has landed

SHAKEN AND STIRRED (MONDAY, DECEMBER 3)

As I enter the final month of the year my emotions feel like they've been shaken vigorously up and down in one of those chrome cocktail makers by an over-enthusiastic barman. One ingredient In this cocktail is the thrill of seeing the early signs of success of our sausage plan. Many of the stores who had reserved promotional slots for our pizzas have switched these to our sausages. Naturalness and authenticity are hot topics at the moment for the supermarkets, so they really liked our new original recipe range. But the biggest surprise was the reaction to Brian's You Tube video with Laura's tips on getting the family eating together. It had started off slowly, like a plane taxiing along the runway. Then suddenly, it had climbed and soared skywards, and had been viewed by an eye-popping 50 000 people. It seems that the whole idea of Simpton's Sunday had hit a real nerve with people.

However, mixed in with this positive feeling is a nagging worry about my future. My 12 months as a CROFTer are almost up and I don't know what the New Year will hold for me job-wise. Tessa has the Sales Director's role for sure, and even going back to my old job looks unlikely given my spurning of Andy Nichol's offer to go back to Sales early. My prospects in the marketing department were of course even gloomier, with Hugo counting down the days until he gets rid of me. Only yesterday I saw him having a blazing row in his office with Marcus Evans from HR. My guess is that Hugo was trying to kick me out right now, whilst Marcus wanted to keep me for a few extra weeks while they figure out my redundancy package. To rub my nose in the pile of manure I've fallen into, I got a Xmas card from William Dawson the headhunter, saying what a shame it was I hadn't taken the Tesco job. And I'm not the only one who is worried. Jane, Brian and Shelly are horrified at the prospect of having Hugo back as their direct boss. The only one who is happy at the moment is Claire. She's blissfully unaware that I'll probably be out of a job in a matter of weeks, and I haven't plucked up the courage to tell her the truth yet. With two lots of school fees and a mortgage to pay, not to mention the kitchen extension that she's launched into, I know I should be looking for a new job, but the job market's pretty much closed down now, with the Xmas party season fully underway.

FIVE MINUTES OF FAME (MONDAY, DECEMBER 10)

I had my five minutes of fame today when I was interviewed on breakfast TV. That's right, Bob the TV star. The You Tube video was picked up by a journalist at the TV company and they wanted to do a feature about our Simpton's Sunday campaign. They even played an excerpt from the video on national TV before I came on, which meant that another few million people got to see it. The team at the office thoroughly enjoyed the whole thing, and spent the rest of the day making fun of me, asking for autographs and offering to powder my nose. We were also seeing a stream of resulting traffic to our website and, most importantly, the feedback from the sales team was good. By getting the brand's name out there more people were picking us off the shelf when they went shopping. And I was confident that Ron's work on the product would mean that people would come back for more after tasting the sausages.

DIARY OF A DOOMED MAN (FRIDAY, DECEMBER 14)

Today I wrote a list of what I'd learnt during my time in brand management, in an attempt to convince myself that the year had not been a total waste of time that had de-railed my career and put my family's financial future in jeopardy. Unfortunately, this was like trying to clean my multi-storey car park of depression with an old toothbrush.

You have to cut through the bull and buzzwords of branding: people like Hugo and Kitty get branding a bad name by making it much more complicated than it needs to be, with jargon, buzzwords and pyramids. I even fell into this trap with the first pub test of our brand ideas.

A brand is more than an image wrapper: branding is not just about logos and fancy advertising. A brand is something people know and trust to deliver a certain experience, and you have to deliver on the promise you make in everything you do. Break this promise and you lose the trust of your consumers, and it's downhill from there on. This is where we went wrong when we started to cut quality bit by bit, at the same time as the retailers were upping their game.

Great brands have sausage and sizzle: relying too much on emotional sizzle is a recipe for disaster, as shown by our failed pizza launch. The best brands have a great product and keep working at making this better and better, whilst also having emotional appeal that builds off this.

Avoid brand ego trips: brands should remember what made them famous, and stick to what they're good at. They should avoid brand ego trips where they go off into new markets that add nothing new, like easyGroup trying to do cinemas and shaving foam. Focus innovation on growing your main business, making what is strong even stronger.

Be **the consumer:** true insight doesn't come from focus groups, or any research come to that. It comes from diving deep into the real world of your consumers, so you get an emotional feeling in your gut, not just a rational understanding. Best of all: hire people who are actually consumers of the product.

Brand vision is a journey, not a box-filling exercise: I saw how dry and complex the original vision for Simpton's was after the box-filling exercise was carried out. We got something more inspiring by using exercises to make us think about what we wanted to fight for, and then summarizing the answers in a simple tool.

Think less, do more: inventing ideas, such as products and promotions, to bring the vision to life helped us understand it as a team and made exploring the vision with consumers much easier.

Show them the money: senior management and other functions like Sales and Finance want to see how your brand plans are going to drive growth. They think branding is all smoke and mirrors, so you have to demonstrate the bottom line benefits.

Make the most of the whole marketing mix: having no budget forces you to be creative and see how to use everything you can to communicate, as shown by The Geek Squad.

Don't brand-wash people: engagement is not about what you say, it's about what you do. Actions speak louder than words. This means having a product people feel proud of, hiring the right people and then linking rewards to doing the right stuff. Brand leaders then need to lead by example. And avoid rapping at all cost.

Marketing is about making money, not movies: communication should tell a product story with emotional appeal, not be an exercise in sponsored entertainment. Start with a big Idea and then see how to execute in different channels, rather than starting with TV as the answer.

What a bummer that I won't get a chance to apply this learning next year.

WALKING THE PLANK (WEDNESDAY, DECEMBER 19)

My worries about next year almost became academic today at the company Xmas party, as I almost collapsed with a cardiac arrest. Never have I lived through such a roller-coaster of emotions.

The day had started with a trip around the factory, with Ron leading the way, beaming like a proud father. The place was buzzing with activity as the team tried to keep up with the sudden surge in sausage demand. We then had a slap-up lunch in the canteen. I noticed that Hugo was missing, but then he never was a fan of factory trips.

I could see Old Mr Simpton talking to the Sales Director, Andy Nichols, who had an earnest look on his face and was solemnly shaking his head. This was it. I was going to get the chop. And after all I had done this year. Those words of the Pet Shop Boys came back to haunt me again... 'What have I, what have I, what have I done to deserve this?' Penny, Simpton's blue-rinsed PA, came up to me and sternly announced that her boss passed on his apologies that he would not be able to talk to me in person before making his announcements to the whole company.

Old Mr Simpton stepped up onto the stage and coughed to clear his throat. The room fell silent, and all I could hear was the whirring of the heating fans placed in the corner to warm up the factory. The speech started with heartfelt thanks to all the people in the factory who had worked night and day to keep up with demand and ship a record month's sales of sausages. The future of the company was safe if we kept this up. This was met with raucous applause, cat whistles and much patting on the back. Old Mr Simpton then announced that he was coming out of retirement to take back the role of Chairman, with his nephew going back to the City where he belonged. He said that if Rupert Murdoch was young enough to still be in business, then so was he. The noise level got even louder and the crowd rose to give a standing ovation.

The second bit of news confirmed my worst fears. Andy Nichols was going to spend even more time on the golf course from now on. The Sales Director chair would be amply filled by Tessa Williams. She caught my eye and winked with a satisfied grin. The plotting she had done with Hugo at Soho House had paid off big time for her, it seemed.

Old Mr Simpton moved on to congratulate the marketing team on coming up with a creative and highly effective campaign that had saved the day. He then said he had an announcement to make about the team. I would no longer be working as the Marketing Manager. I gulped, wondering how to tell Claire that we have to cancel the ski trip and send the extension builders home. It was at least nice to hear a few other people whisper protests and surprise at this news. I started to make my way out of the crowd, weaving past people, drunk with the news of my impending doom. But my progress was stopped by Old Mr Simpton booming that he hadn't done with me yet. Then suddenly, people around me were laughing and smiling, and I was being clapped heartily on the back. Were people this happy to see me go? Then I heard Old Mr Simpton repeat his final announcement, and only then did the reality start to sink in. 'Please join me In congratulating Bob. Our new Marketing Director!'

HUGO GOES HUGE (FRIDAY, DECEMBER 21)

When we got back to the office after the Xmas party we found that Hugo's office was empty apart from the broken-framed portrait of Brandy. I felt sad for a second, until Shelly broken the silence by announcing 'Good riddance to the tosser'. We wondered what Hugo would do after Simpton's and found the answer on the front page of today's *Marketing* magazine. He is launching a new-age brand consultancy called Hugbrands in partnership with Kitty from ETC. The consultancy will take all the Hugbrand thinking behind the Simpsational pizza work and help clients apply it to their businesses. With a bit of luck they'll go and work for our competitors.

Amazingly, we'll only be 2% below our sales target for the year. The first full month of sausage sales are up 30% versus last year, and have almost made up for the shortfall from the failed pizza launch. The good news is that we will just scrape our profit target as we make more money on the sausages. The real test will be the first market share results we get in January to see how consumer sales are going. And we then need to create a stream of new ideas to ensure the re-launch is not just a one-hit wonder.

The phone didn't stop ringing all day with people calling up to congratulate me and in some cases already start sniffing for business. I took great pleasure in asking Shelly to tell INK and ETC that I was busy and would get back to them in the New Year. Perhaps. But the most amusing call of the day was from a professor called Mark Ritson who teaches at London Business School, where Hugo did his MBA. He asked me to come and do a talk next year about the Simpton's re-launch on his brand management course. It only seems like five minutes ago that Hugo was chastising me for my lack of an MBA during the Babbington House workshop. Perhaps he'd like to come and listen to the talk?

Index